"MAGIC"

A BIOGRAPHY OF
Earvin Johnson

by
JAMES HASKINS

ENSLOW PUBLISHERS
Bloy Street and Ramsey Avenue
Box 777
Hillside, New Jersey 07205

PART 1

High School

working what amounted to three jobs herself just taking care of all those children. Earvin and his brothers and sisters learned early to take care of themselves, but they never felt unloved. Somehow, in spite of the burdens and pressures on them, Earvin and Christine Johnson managed to create a loving, close-knit atmosphere in their home, and they are surely responsible for its continued closeness, even though several children are now out on their own. As Earvin says, "Kids should be close to their families, because the family is always behind you."

Earvin, Jr.'s strong "team-concept" about basketball may have started with his family. With so many children, it was important that the older ones learn responsibility early. They had to help out with the younger children, and they had to learn how to take care of themselves. They learned that everybody had to help out, and as soon as they were able, even the littlest Johnson children had small chores to do around the house.

At the same time, the Johnson children were also taught that they were needed and wanted not just because they were family but because they were individuals. Mrs. Johnson says, "One thing Earvin was taught was to be himself." When he showed a special liking for music, he was encouraged to pursue it. He got a transistor radio for Christmas, and from then on he rarely went anywhere without it. And when it wore out from so much use, his parents made sure he got another one. Earvin had a fine singing voice, too. After his voice changed in adolescence and he still had a good singing voice, Mrs. Johnson, for one, started thinking that her son might be able to have a singing career.

Growing up in such a big family, Earvin, Jr., also grew up liking people. He was outgoing from the start and curious about the world around him. As a youngster he was popular in the neighborhood. Later, when he started school, he was popular there, too. He seems to have been born with that infectious grin and happy-go-lucky attitude that makes him so popular with basketball fans today.

Earvin and the other Johnson boys were introduced to basketball early. Both their parents had been basketball players when they were younger. Mrs. Johnson had played high school basketball in her hometown in North Carolina, and Mr. Johnson had played in his hometown of Brookhaven, Mississippi. During basketball season, whenever he got a chance, Mr. Johnson would watch professional games on television. His children would join him, and he would explain how the game was played.

Mr. Johnson would point out things like how guard Oscar Robertson would take a smaller guard underneath, or the pick and roll. In this way, the Johnson children learned the finer points of the game. By the time Earvin started playing organized ball, if the coach asked whether anybody knew how to do a three-man weave or a left-handed lay-up, he was the first one up.

By the time Larry was in fifth grade and Earvin was in fourth, the Johnson brothers were getting up early on Sunday mornings to go one-on-one in full-court games at the nearby Main Street Elementary School playground. Earvin says he had to learn to dribble because his brother pressed him baseline-to-baseline all the time.

The boys didn't play as Larry and Earvin Johnson. They played as basketball superstars. Larry's hero was Walt Frazier, the young scoring guard with the New York Knicks. Earvin's was Wilt Chamberlain, the giant center for the Los Angeles Lakers. Little did the two Johnson boys know that one day Earvin would play on the same team as had his first hero —except that he would not play center. In fact, Earvin would

of experience, and thanks to his father, a pretty thorough knowledge of the game.

By the time Earvin went on to Dwight Rice Junior High School, he had grown to be six feet tall, but almost all of his growth was up. He was very, very skinny. He was not a powerful athlete, but he had remarkable coordination considering that he had a body that could very easily have gotten out of control because it was growing so fast. He tried out for and made the football team as well as the basketball team and according to his high school coach, George Fox, was outstanding at both games. But he was especially good at basketball. He did not score all that much, but he was an excellent passer, and he seemed to have a better sense of what was happening on court than other boys his age. What's more, he played basketball with a total joy that was infectious. He made the game more fun for his teammates.

People who knew basketball began to notice Earvin when he was still in junior high. He once went to the intramural building at Michigan State University in nearby East Lansing. The MSU star Terry Furlow, who was playing there at the time, noticed the tall, skinny kid and asked him to play. Earvin hadn't been expecting that. He'd just come to watch. He was very nervous when he went out on the court, but his playing didn't show it. Furlow started calling Earvin his "main man." The MSU star became Earvin's hero. He tried to play like him, and he tried to act like him. Furlow had great "charisma," which means that people were naturally attracted to him. He was usually the "life of the party" off court, the star of the game on the basketball floor.

While he was still in junior high school, Earvin also first came into contact with Dr. Charles Tucker, a clinical psychologist and part-time teacher at Michigan State University who worked part-time as a psychological counselor for the Lansing school district. Tucker had been a pro basketball player and had spent a year and a half with the Memphis franchise of the American Basketball Association. He was interested in Earvin, and Earvin was in awe of anyone who had actually been with the pros. Over time, Tucker came to know the Johnson family and became an unofficial adviser to Earvin.

Another man who would become important to Earvin was George Fox, the basketball coach at Everett High School in Lansing, who naturally was interested in the local junior high talent. Fox still remembers the first time he saw Earvin play: "He was six-foot three and 125 pounds and couldn't dribble," he says with a laugh. At that time Earvin was so tall and gangly he looked awkward on the floor. Still, there was that passing skill and an indefinable quality that made Fox and other high school coaches pay close attention to him. "We were well aware in junior high school that he'd be all-state some day," Fox recalls.

George Fox did not think he would ever coach Earvin Johnson because in those days Everett High was 98 percent white, as a result of its location in the white southeast section of the city. The school was about a mile and a half from Earvin's home on Middle Street in the inner city near the Oldsmobile factory. George Fox, and Earvin Johnson, thought Earvin would be going to Sexton High, about one-half mile from his home and almost all black. When Earvin was in ninth grade, the Lansing school board redistricted its population to bring about integration. To his dismay, Earvin learned that he would be bused to Everett High.

"I was upset," Earvin told Mike O'Hara of the *Detroit News*. "I wanted to go to Sexton. I went to every Sexton game. I was a Sexton man, and then they came up with this busing thing."

Fox said, "I was very pleased when after about two days he turned it back in. He wasn't physically strong enough to play football. I was also very glad that he didn't pursue baseball or any other sports."

Fox wasted no time going to work with his team. He added a new dimension to his coaching that year. He introduced a lot more drills—primarily reaction drills—to increase his players' timing, quickness, and overall agility. Earvin responded well to these drills and, in George Fox's opinion, "This was the best thing I did for Earvin. We had countless timing and reaction drills to work on his defense. He liked to help out on defense and we encouraged him to play more honest and not so top-heavy. He stood up a lot, and he had probably tried to use his height to too much advantage at a younger age."

Practicing with the team helped Earvin to adjust to his new school, because it helped him to feel as if he belonged. Still that first year at Everett was not easy for him. Although the busing program brought more blacks to Everett, they remained only a small part of the total school population. For a young black man who'd grown up in a black neighborhood and spent all his previous school years in almost completely black schools, simply attending an integrated school was a new experience indeed.

Going to a new, mostly white, school wasn't the only problem Earvin was having at the time. He was also going through the same difficulties that complicate most teenagers' lives when they find that they don't quite fit in either the world of children or the world of adults.

Added to this, Earvin's parents, especially his mother, were very strict. As Charles Tucker puts it, "She didn't let Earvin get away with anything." Earvin felt as if his parents were treating him like a kid when it was very clear, to him at least, that he was growing up. He felt like rebelling against their strictness. He didn't feel that they understood him at all.

George Fox remembers, "Back in the early 70s, when I first met Earvin, society was a little more turbulent. [Because of the busing situation] there were reflections of racism around, and I don't think Earvin was as pleasant a person when I met him as he was after he blossomed into a more mature individual. He was a little moody and sulky and he would become despondent over little things. If I could take some credit for helping him off the court I would say that I helped him in his progress toward maturity by encouraging him not to be despondent over little things and to be very respectful toward his parents because they are strong, good people. I'd say, 'Earvin, stay humble,' and I told him that quite a lot. He still kids me a little bit about that. He uses the word himself a lot now."

Basketball has been good for Earvin Johnson in many ways, not the least of which was helping him to get through some difficult growing-up years. The tall, skinny kid with the huge Afro who first walked through the doors of Everett High not knowing what to expect or what was expected of him became one of the most popular students in the school. Before long his smile grew as big as his Afro.

Earvin's first friend at Everett High was Reggie Chastine, a basketball teammate. The 5-foot-6-inch guard, who was a year ahead of Earvin, also had come to Everett as a result of the busing program. His basketball "philosophy" was like Earvin's. He enjoyed ball-handling, making lots of assists, and he had fun playing the game. He also liked music and other people.

The pair who had a lot in common except for their size became a familiar sight at Everett High. They became even more familiar to the other students once the basketball season began.

greatest number of assists with 138 (Reggie Chastine's total was next highest at 103 and senior Dan Parks was third with 66). Another highest total was a little bit embarrassing for Earvin— 75 violations (Reggie Chastine had the next highest with 63)— but Earvin reasoned that if you were going to play aggressive ball, you were going to have to commit a lot of fouls. That high statistic didn't bother Coach Fox either. He remembered that just a year before, his young star had spent a lot of time standing around, waiting for the ball to come to him.

Earvin wasn't content to rest on his statistics. He spent the summer improving his own basketball as well as that of others. Charles Tucker operated "Dr. Tucker's Basketball Camp" in Lansing during the summer, and Earvin worked there as an instructor. Michigan State star Terry Furlow, who had led the Big Ten in scoring that season, was an instructor at the camp, too. Earvin and Terry spent every spare moment going one-on-one. In an all-star game at the camp Earvin scored 26 points. He wasn't even 17 years old yet.

Chapter 2

By the beginning of his junior year, Earvin had settled in happily at Everett High. The main reason was basketball. He liked his coach and his teammates—he had found his best and closest friend, Reggie Chastine, through basketball.

But there was more to him than just basketball playing. He had other friends. Coach Fox recalls, "His best friends were basically other members of the team, but Earvin always had a few other young men hanging around him that he identified with that were not basketball players."

He didn't just ride on his celebrity as a basketball player. He got involved in other aspects of life at Everett High and was liked as a person, too. "Earvin was very popular with both the faculty and the students," says George Fox. "He wasn't strong in the college aptitude-type science and math courses, but in human relations and human behavior and those types of courses, he excelled."

Earvin was not a great student, but he got by. His parents, especially his mother, would have been very upset if he hadn't gotten passing grades. They wanted him to go to college, and because he was a fine athlete they realized he could get the

record of 21-1 and a league record of 12-0, were once again league champions, and once again they had a chance to go all the way to the state Class A title. The game for the regional championship was no contest at all: Everett beat Niles High by 40 points. Victory against their next opponent, Battle Creek High, was a little less certain, but the final score was 66-55, making the Vikings regional champs for the second year in a row.

They next met Detroit Northeastern, the only team that had beaten them in the regular season. The game was played at the Jackson Parkside High School gym in Jackson, Michigan—the same gym where Everett had lost to Fordson High of Dearborn in the quarterfinals the year before. The big crowd of 4,500 that jammed the arena saw the Vikings play some fine basketball for the first half of the game while they built up a 15-point lead. But then the Vikings seemed to lose their momentum. Soon it looked as if they were going to do the same thing as they had the previous year—blow a big lead and lose. When the second half began, Northeastern seemed to regroup and begin to chip away at the Vikings' lead. By early in the fourth quarter, Northeastern had pulled to within three points. The score was 48-45 but Everett came back with seven straight free throws, four by Larry Hunter, two by Earvin, and one by Paul Dawson, which brought the score to 55-46.

Northeastern went on a shooting spree, outscoring Everett 8-2. "It was only fitting," said the reporter for the *Detroit News*, "that Everett's outstanding 6-foot-7 junior forward, Earvin Johnson, who played a superb all-around game, came

---

Earvin Johnson stands with his close friend Reggie Chastine.

Brian Burd, Lansing State Journal

Considering the huge differences between his totals and those of the next best players, it is little wonder that Earvin blamed himself for the loss to Detroit Catholic Central. On the other hand, when he blamed himself he was forgetting that although he might be the star he was still just one member of a team. He had yet to realize that when you play a team sport—win or lose—the result belongs to every member.

That summer Earvin's friend and teammate Reggie Chastine was killed in an automobile accident. Reggie and a girl friend were driving in Jackson one evening when the car Reggie was driving was struck broadside at an intersection by another auto. Reggie's girl was not hurt, nor were the 17-year-old driver of the other car and his three passengers. But Reggie died in the hospital an hour later.

The news shocked the people of Lansing, especially the kids and teachers at Everett High. But of all the people at Everett, Earvin Johnson was most deeply affected. "That young man was Earvin's best and closest friend," says George Fox.

Reggie's death didn't just make Earvin sad. It caused him to do a lot of thinking. The same thing could have happened to anyone, he realized. *The same thing could happen to me.*

No radical change came over Earvin Johnson as a result of his friend's death. It was his natural way to love life and people and to live each day to its fullest. But after Reggie's death he had an even greater sense of appreciation for the gift of being alive.

Chapter 3

Despite the tragedy of Reggie's death, life started getting pretty exciting for Earvin Johnson during the spring and summer of 1976. Any high school player who is named to that many first teams, as well as best-this and most-that, starts to get a lot of attention. People who were in a position to know were saying that he was the best prospect to come out of Michigan in years and, probably, among the top five high school players in the whole country. He was already getting five or six letters from colleges every day. Since he hadn't even started his senior year of high school yet, the pace of attention was sure to increase as the months wore on.

Detroit News reporter Mike O'Hara got hold of a copy of the Bill Cronauer Scouting Service report on Earvin. Many college athletic departments subscribe to this service, and this is what it had to say about the Everett star: "This is the man! He's a 6-7 (now 6-8, going on 6-9) who plays like a 6'3" guard. Downtown shooting range, so effortless. Can pick a shot out of the air, then take it the length of the floor and score."

Bird of Indiana State and Johnson and Kelser of MSU in the 1979 NCAA championship game.   *Michigan State University*

The college scouts and coaches themselves pretty much agreed with the scouting service reports. But there was something else they were looking for—a good attitude—and Earvin Johnson had it. "A coach told me that because of his attitude it must be nice working with a superstar who's not on an ego trip," says George Fox. "He not only had personal goals but he also had team goals. We'd run through fundamental drills and he, a high school All-American, would enjoy them."

Earvin liked all the attention he was getting because it showed he was good at what he did. He didn't get a swelled head about it all, which made him even more attractive to the college coaches. They were looking for another player on their team, not a one-man team. But Earvin was only human, and he couldn't help being affected by it all. He began to have wonderful dreams. In one, he went right from high school to the pros with a three-year, million-dollar contract and, by the time he woke up, he was Rookie of the Year. In another, he was riding around Lansing with recruiters—in Cadillacs. When he told the adults around him about these dreams, they realized it was time to start getting him to focus on reality.

Mrs. Johnson was kind of wistful about the situation. She had always wanted her son to try for a singing career—after he finished college. She thought he was awfully young to be the object of so much attention, and besides, this recruiting business was threatening to disrupt the life of her family.

Mr. Johnson and Dr. Tucker, who was called in as a family adviser, agreed that it wasn't good for Earvin to be in the spotlight so much. Earvin's coach, George Fox, found himself in the limelight, too, and it made him uncomfortable. The coach of a high-school superstar often either gets a chance to join the athletic department of the chosen college or becomes a prime candidate for a coaching position at some other college. But George Fox wasn't interested in riding anywhere on his young star's coattails. "I didn't want anything from him and he didn't want anything from me," he states. "I told him once that someday we could sit down and he could buy me a steak dinner. He thought that was great."

Fox, Tucker, and the Johnsons got together and laid down some early and firm ground rules. There would be no open season on Earvin Johnson. They would choose seven or eight schools in which Earvin was really interested. The rest would be turned down politely. Earvin said he thought his initial list should include UCLA, Louisville, Michigan, North Carolina

State, Marquette, Notre Dame, Indiana, and Michigan State. The others said fine, and so in the next few weeks George Fox said "No, thank you," on Earvin's behalf, to Western Michigan, Duke, and a number of other colleges.

Meanwhile, Earvin became managing editor of the high school newspaper his senior year. "I like to write," he explained. He also found that he enjoyed selling advertising space, because it meant getting out and meeting and talking with people. Needless to say, he was very successful at that job, for local merchants knew his reputation and were pleased to buy space in the paper from Everett's star athlete. He also continued to volunteer his time at the two local Boys Clubs, teaching basketball to youngsters. Recently, he'd been named Boys Club Boy of the Year.

He turned down election as president of Lansing's Junior National Association for the Advancement of Colored People (NAACP) because he knew that playing basketball would not allow him to devote as much time as he should to the office, but he continued to be an active member. "You get to meet people you'd never get to meet—congressmen, important people," he told Mike O'Hara of the *Detroit News*. "You learn so much about different things." On top of all this, he was carrying a B average in his courses—without any help from friendly teachers.

Earvin liked to be active and involved. Although he had always been this way, he had become even more so since the death of Reggie Chastine. Just because he'd been getting a whole lot of attention lately, Earvin had not forgotten his friend. In fact, as basketball season approached, the Viking's "tri-captain" (with Paul Dawson and Larry Hunter) dedicated his senior season to Reggie, and his teammates followed suit. They solemnly promised one another that this year they were going to win the state title for Reggie. The vow put a lot of pressure on them. And, they were already under quite a bit of pressure, for with All-American Earvin Johnson on the team, as Coach Fox put it, "It's not just enough for us to win. We have to win big."

In Earvin Johnson's opinion, a high school basketball rule change made that year might help them to win big. After 10 years, the dunk shot was finally made legal again. This was one of Earvin's favorite playground moves, and it was a great crowd-pleaser. When Earvin heard the news that the dunk was legal again, he was in school. He jumped up and down and ran through the halls yelling for joy. In no time everyone at Everett High knew that the dunk was back.

George Fox also realized the importance of the dunk shot in the coming season. If the Vikings were supposed to dazzle their opponents, he'd add a dazzling new play. A guard would steal the ball and go in as if for a lay-up while Earvin trailed behind. But instead of bouncing the ball off the backboard and into the basket, the guard would bounce it off the glass back to Earvin, who would dunk it. It was called the "Glass Shot."

Perhaps Earvin had heard his coach say that with him on the team the Vikings would be expected to win big. Perhaps he thought he was playing for both himself and Reggie Chastine. Perhaps he couldn't help romping over opponents who were no match for him, and perhaps all the attention he'd been getting had gone to his head just a little bit. Whatever the reason, Earvin Johnson started out the Vikings' 1976-77 season as if he'd forgotten all about the team concept that made him so attractive to college coaches around the nation.

Coach Fox recalls, "After the first four games of his senior year, he was averaging over 40 points a game. I called him in and said, 'If we're going to win the state, you can't continue to play the way you're playing. You've got the entire crowd watching you, and the opponents all watching you, and that's fine. But you've also got four teammates watching you. You're going to have to start letting your teammates get involved.' Earvin said, 'I got you coach.' The next game he scored 12 points and had 18 assists. That's the kind of person he is."

In their first 14 games, the Everett team won by an *average* of 39 points. The average would have been over 40 points if Eastern High hadn't given the Vikings a real run for the money in their third game of the season.

The game dedicated Eastern's brand-new, 4,500-seat gym. A sellout crowd saw Eastern force Everett into overtime before it could come up with an 86-79 victory. Earvin's leg was heavily taped because of an injury he suffered in an earlier game against Howell, but that didn't prevent him from scoring 45 points and grabbing 30 rebounds.

After the game, Coach Fox told reporter Mike O'Hara, "If he played on a different team, and played guard and had the ball . . . it scares me. He could average 45, 50 points a game. He could average as many as he wanted to. Even if you played some combination defense, you'd foul him all the time. We're restricting him, and he restricts himself, because if we're going to win the state championship, we have to play total basketball."

Fox recognized the danger in so many big wins. His players could easily start getting sloppy because they had so little competition. Fox urged his team to pay attention to performance, not to the score. "We'd take pride in not letting a team make a lay-up all night. Things like that—the challenge. We knew we were going to win."

When the Vikings lost to Eastern by eight points in their fifteenth game, they dropped to the Number 2 spot in state ranking. But soon they were back up at Number 1, and there would be no more losses for them during the regular season. There would just be more spectacular wins behind the dazzling play of Earvin Johnson. As what George Fox calls a "whirlwind season" wore on, sportswriters used up all their superlative adjectives to describe Johnson. Until now, they had avoided using Fred Stabley, Jr.'s, nickname, but now they couldn't resist, and soon just about everyone called him "Magic" Johnson.

In no time at all, the state tournaments had rolled around again. The Vikings had sworn to go all the way this time, and they made their resolve very convincing as they romped past their opponents 64-44 and 86-57 to win the regional finals and the quarterfinals. In the semifinals they beat Saginaw High 48-40. All that remained was one more game, this one against Birmingham's Brother Rice High, which had beaten Detroit Catholic Central in the other semifinal match.

It was one of the toughest games the Vikings had ever played. Both teams played superbly, and at the end of regulation time the score was tied at 49-all, forcing them into a three-minute extra period. No one scored for the first minute and eight seconds. Then Magic was fouled. He made the free throw, and his teammate, Dale Beard, followed it with a field goal. Rice brought the ball upcourt, shot, and missed. Magic grabbed the rebound, raced the length of the court, made a crowd-pleasing behind-the-back dribble, and scored. When he fouled out 8 seconds later, the crowd gave him a standing ovation. He had played "magically" to gain totals of 34 points, 14 rebounds, 4 assists. Everett fans started chanting, "Earvin Johnson! Earvin Johnson!" They kept it up as the clock wound down.

Meanwhile, the game continued. "When Earvin fouled out with 1:03 left on the clock, and we had a five-point lead, I was still very much concerned," Coach Fox recalls. "But the other players, especially a young man named James Huffman, came through for us." The final score was 62-56.

For a few minutes, the Vikings and their fans went wild, jumping up and down, hugging each other, and screaming, "We're number 1!" But the Number 1 player on the Number 1 team grew quiet after a time. He was thinking of Reggie Chastine. "Reggie played a big part in my life and that's why the team and I dedicated this state championship to him," Earvin told *Detroit News* reporter Mike O'Hara. "Before each game this season, we held one or two minutes of silence as a memorial to Reggie. I definitely feel he was part of us winning the state championship."

Of course, Earvin "Magic" Johnson played a big part in that win himself. In the 28 games he'd played since the season began, he had scored 805 points for an average of 28.75 points per game. He had pulled down 469 rebounds for an average of 16.75. He'd made 208 assists and 99 steals. He had made the all-state team again to become the first three-time all-state player in Michigan history.

This time, UPI had named him "Prep Player of the Year" not just for Michigan but for the whole country. But still, in George Fox's opinion, Earvin had not won the national attention he deserved. "Some high school All-American teams didn't even have him on their top 25 for his senior year," says Fox, "and I wrote a couple of those magazines and asked why. I never received a reply from those sports editors, so maybe they were embarrassed about it."

At Coach Fox's urging, Earvin had tried not to star so much that year, but instead to be more of a team player. He started out averaging over 40 points a game. By the end of the season his average was just under 29 points per game. He may have suffered as a result of his unselfishness—at least in terms of honors and national recognition—but in the years to come he would be grateful to his high school coach for constantly reminding him to "stay humble."

Looking back, Fox was better able than most people to see how Earvin Johnson developed into a star player: "Earvin, from the first time we started coaching him, was an outstanding player. But he wasn't physically strong enough to do the things he wanted to do—and could do—mentally. If he hadn't put on a lot of weight and gotten a lot stronger, he would not have developed as he did.

"I would say that in his junior-year tournaments he really started to emerge. He did more and more things all the time. His passing was phenomenal, especially his outlet passing. He was so good that our opponents started to front him all the time on his rebounds. We had to make a few changes because of this. We'd have him dump the ball off, and then we'd have the guards give it back to him when he cut by them. It took a while for his college coaches and even his pro coaches to realize how he was at ball handling. Bringing the ball down the court is the best thing he does, and I think it surprises everybody that he did the same thing in high school."

Happy as he was about that 1977 state tournament win, Coach Fox (and everyone else at Everett High) was sort of wistful about the end of basketball season that year. It would be a long time before a player like Earvin Johnson would come their way again.

Now that his high school basketball career was over, Earvin had to choose where he would make his college career. Back in the fall, before basketball season began, he had visited four colleges—Michigan, Notre Dame, North Carolina State, and Maryland. Under the rules of the National Collegiate Athletic Association, he was eligible to visit two more, but by January he was weary of it all. Believe it or not, he cancelled a planned visit to the University of Southern California that month because he was actually tired of free plane rides, being chauffeured around in limousines, being wined and dined, meeting coaches and college stars, and being told how much he was wanted. His cheeks were normally well-exercised from smiling, but after one of those visits he'd be so tired from smiling that his whole face would hurt.

"At first you like it, you love it," he told a *Detroit News* reporter. "It's a dream to be recruited. But after it gets going, it gets bad. There are telephone calls, and it gets to be a hassle."

Of course, it hadn't been much of a hassle to visit Michigan State University over in East Lansing. He already knew it well because of Dr. Tucker and Terry Furlow, who had been drafted by the Philadelphia 76ers in 1976 and then been traded to the Cleveland Cavaliers in 1977. Still, there was a lot of pressure on him to go to MSU, especially from MSU fans. When the Michigan Wolverines came to MSU for a game in January, some of the MSU fans even brought along signs that said, "We want Earvin." Nearly everywhere he went in Lansing, people would urge Earvin to stay in his home town so they could continue to watch him play.

By the time the Everett Vikings had won the state Class A championship, the list of colleges had been narrowed down to two—the University of Michigan in Ann Arbor and Michigan State. Earvin had decided that he didn't really want to go too far away from home and that he'd be happier in a school in the state, which meant going to either U.M. or MSU.

Before he made his decision, Earvin made his first trip to Europe. With other American high school all-stars, he went to Germany to play in the Albert Schweitzer games. It was a great experience for him, and it gave him a chance to escape the pressure on him to choose a college. But the pressure started to build again as soon as he got off the plane that brought him home. A huge crowd was waiting to welcome him. Half of them were waving University of Michigan banners, the other half had MSU banners.

There were long and intense talks with people in the athletic departments of both schools. Earvin found that he liked them all, but he especially liked MSU's assistant basketball coach, Vern Payne. When it was announced in the middle of April that Payne was leaving MSU to become the first black head-coach of basketball at Wayne State, many people wondered if it would affect Earvin's decision. University of Michigan officials thought it might, and even before Payne's move was officially announced they were trying to find out for sure. More calls were made to the Johnsons just in case the University of Michigan's chances would be increased because of Payne's departure from MSU.

In the end, Payne's leaving did not matter. Earvin chose Michigan State anyway. He chose it because it was in his hometown, and because of the basketball experience he could get there. The University of Michigan had a far better basketball program than MSU had. MSU's program had practically fallen apart a couple of years back, when the school had been involved in a scandal concerning special favors to athletes. Since then, the new coach, Jud Heathcote, had been trying to rebuild the program, but that kind of rebuilding took time.

Most athletes faced with the choice of a school with a winning basketball team and one with a losing team naturally want to be on the winning side. Earvin Johnson was no exception. He leaned toward the University of Michigan, but his father wanted him to go to Michigan State. After he got used to the idea, Earvin kind of liked the prospect of playing on an underdog team and helping it to change from being a losing to a winning five. He'd done that at Everett; it would be a challenge to see if he could do it at MSU. Besides, he would enjoy more playing time with a team that did not have a lot of already established stars. And, finally, he would be able to play with his friend, Jay Vincent, who already had decided to go to MSU. At Eastern High, Jay had made a name for himself, just as Earvin had done at Everett.

At the end of April 1977, Earvin Johnson signed a "national letter of intent" to go to MSU. The great recruiting blitz of his senior year ended at last. He hoped the final weeks of his senior year and his summer would be filled with something other than basketball.

In May Earvin was invited to the annual Michigan Roundball Classic at the University of Detroit. He had planned to go, but then he found out that the classic was scheduled for the same time as his prom pictures. Earvin stood up the classic. There would be many more basketball classics, he decided, but there would only be one high school senior prom.

PART 2

College

Chapter 4 ─────────

Michigan State University was one of the first land-grant colleges in the country. In the middle of the last century Congress voted to donate public lands to be used for colleges that would teach agriculture. The first three states to take advantage of this ruling were Michigan, Pennsylvania, and Illinois. MSU was founded as Michigan Agricultural College in 1855. Its name was changed later when it began to offer courses in other fields besides agriculture. The community that grew up around it was known for over half a century as College Park. In 1907 it was incorporated as a town separate from Lansing, and became known as East Lansing.

Overlooked by the tall Beaumont Tower, the large campus centers around a circular road that is named simply Circle Drive. Students carrying books on just about every subject you can imagine stroll to and fro between the dormitories and classroom buildings.

Although he was going to college in his own hometown, Earvin didn't want to miss out on any part of college life by living at home and commuting to school. He moved into one of the dormitories on campus. That way, he could be on his own, but he could still go home whenever he wanted to, see his family, get his laundry done, and eat a home-cooked meal. It was fun fixing up his room, moving in his stereo and records, putting posters up on the walls.

After he got settled in his new living quarters, it was time to think about his courses. As a freshman, he wouldn't have much choice because there were a lot of required courses in English and math and science that he had to take. He had already decided to major in telecommunications, but he would not be able to start taking courses in that area until his sophomore year, and he would not be able to concentrate on such courses until he was a junior.

On top of his regular course load, he decided to take advantage of what was offered at the college's Learning Resources Center. The center had a speed-reading program and after looking at the reading lists for the courses he had to take, Earvin decided he would need all the help he could get with his reading. "I think that was partly my fault and partly my high school's," he said. "I wasn't really reading back then. When I got in this class, I had a very helpful teacher. She really mapped out some things that were helpful to me."

Earvin decided to study as hard as he could for the first couple of months, because after that he would be so busy with basketball that he wouldn't have as much time to study. His first semester at MSU he got a 3.4 grade average out of a possible 4.0 points.

But he also had fun. He walked around campus with a transistor radio to his ear, smiling and greeting people along the

---

Magic prepares to pass in the 1979 NCAA championship game.

Michigan State University

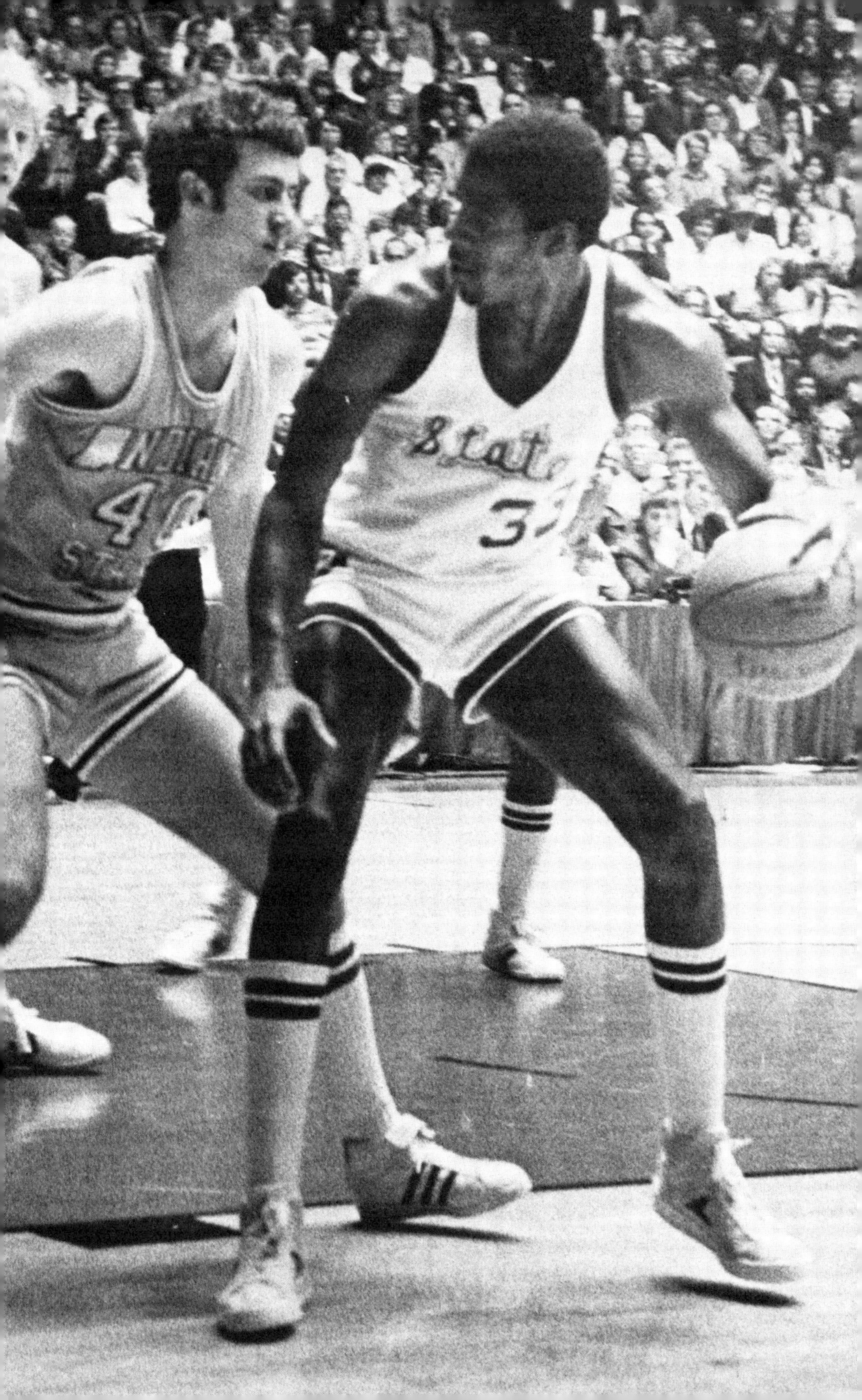
State

way. He went to parties on weekends and dated girls he met and girls he already knew. He even tried his hand at being a disc jockey—at Bonnie and Clyde's in East Lansing—calling himself "E.J. the Deejay."

As the basketball season approached, people would crowd around Earvin and give him words of encouragement about the coming season. Earvin enjoyed being something of a celebrity on campus. "I know I'm a student in a special category," he told Larry Keith, a writer for *Sports Illustrated*. "I mean, I'm a student in the classroom, but around campus I'm Earvin Johnson the basketball player. I can hear people whisper when I walk by, 'Hey, is that Magic?' And I've heard little kids in the playground say, 'I'm Earvin, I'm Earvin.' This is why I'm careful about how I come across to people. I don't want them to think I'm conceited. When you're the main attraction, you've got to watch out."

Actually, it was not hard to be the main attraction in MSU basketball. The school was not exactly noted for its basketball teams. Its last Big Ten titles had come in 1957 and 1959, some 20 years before. Two seasons earlier there had been that big shake-up in the school's athletic department. Jud Heathcote, the former assistant coach at Washington State and head coach at Montana, had arrived as MSU's chief coach in April 1976, just in time to see his new school flop in recruiting. The athletic department had a list of 14 high school basketball players to be recruited. They contacted them all, and were turned down flat by 11 of them. The other three, who showed a little interest, did not bother to visit the school.

Heathcote was supposed to rebuild the basketball program at MSU, but he couldn't do that without talent. By December 1976, with a new basketball season under way and a lousy record, Heathcote was getting tired of being asked when things were going to get better. "When are we going to start seeing some 'firsts'?" someone asked him after a Spartan loss. "Well," said the new coach wryly, "this was the *first* time we've played that team this year, and the *first* time we've been beaten by them this year, and I'm sure there will be other firsts." The Spartans finished the season with a record of 10 and 17.

The successful recruiting of Earvin Johnson was a real feather in Heathcote's cap, and there was a lot of hope for the 1977-78 basketball team. Both Earvin, as point guard, and Jay Vincent, as center, were expected to help junior Greg Kelser. Kelser had been the team's leading scorer and rebounder in the 1976-77 season. Guard Robert Chapman, who was good enough to have been chosen in the fifth round of the NBA draft the previous spring, had decided to stay on at MSU. A lot of people thought he would contribute a lot to the team in the coming season.

Looking over the roster of players, Coach Heathcote saw clear strengths and weaknesses. None of his players was especially strong on defense, but most of them were good scorers. He could work out some defensive patterns for them that would make up for the basic weaknesses on defense, so he was not too worried about that. What did worry him was the possibility that jealousy among his players would prevent them from becoming a real team.

How would Kelser and Chapman feel about Earvin Johnson, this 18-year-old "All-Everything" who had already received more publicity than the two of them put together? "We tried to prepare Greg and Bob for what would happen when the season started," Heathcote told Luther Keith of the *Detroit News*, "and as it turned out the media focused more on Earvin than we had expected."

Greg Kelser, who had gone to high school in Detroit, was Mr. Big on the MSU team. He was the one who had the most reason to be jealous, but he was a calm and serious young man and not one to get upset about something before it happened. Anyway, he had an idea from their first meeting that Earvin wasn't conceited. "I was a senior and he was a sophomore in high school," said Kelser, remembering their first meeting. "I was up at MSU while they were recruiting me, and I met Earvin at a party. I was impressed right away, because he was getting all kinds of press when he was 15 and it didn't swell his head. He was very mature for his age. I realized Earvin was a super player when he came and I figured if we started to win, everything would work out."

The excitement at Jenison Field House the night of the first game of the season was so great you could almost feel it. The old building was packed with 9,886 people who had bought their tickets the April before, as soon as the announcement had come that Earvin Johnson was going to stay in East Lansing. No other freshman basketball player—no other freshman, period—had ever created so much excitement at the school even before he got there. Most of the major newspapers in the state had carried front-page stories with photographs of Earvin that day of the first game—Magic Johnson's debut on the MSU court.

Meanwhile, the object of all this excitement was finally beginning to feel the pressure. He hadn't slept the night before. His stomach was feeling funny. He had barely managed to eat. He was more tense than he had ever been before. While the players on the Central Michigan University team, defending Mid-American Conference champions, were introduced, Earvin took deep breaths to try to steady his racing heart. Then he heard his name called.

Teammate Ron Charles watches Magic complete a dunk in the 1979 NCAA championship game. *Michigan State University*

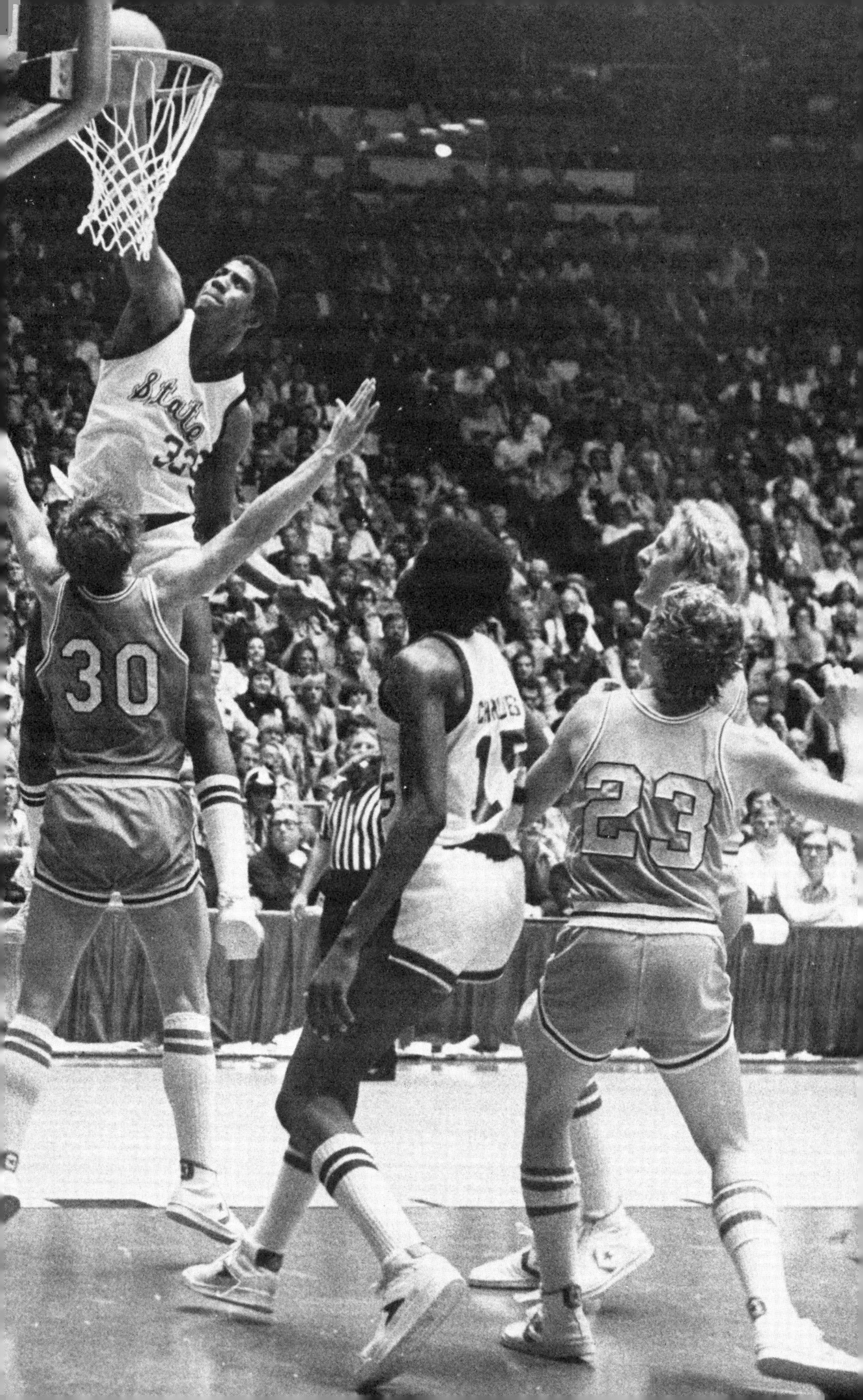
State
30
23

He loped out on the floor and went through the ritual palm-slapping with his teammates as the crowd rose to its feet and began to clap their hands and stomp. Many were wearing bright T-shirts that said "Spartan Spirit." They pointed to their chests and shouted encouragement. They kept up the pounding and cheering all the way through the opening tip and the Spartans' first missed basket—and the second, and the third. Soon it got hard to keep clapping and cheering for a team that wasn't doing anything. The Spartans missed their first *11* shots from the floor; they didn't make a single field goal in the first nine minutes and ten seconds.

The team was "tight." No one was more tense than Earvin, who committed seven turnovers in the first half and couldn't seem to put the ball into the basket either from the floor or from the free-throw line. Luckily, his teammates managed to recover. Greg Kelser found his shooting range and his rebounding ability. Jay Vincent got over his first-game jitters very well. He played the best game of his life, scoring 25 points, 18 of them in the second half, including two crucial three-point plays.

Central Michigan, meanwhile, was not shooting well. The game was close all the way. There were only a couple of minutes left in the game and the Spartans were in the lead 59-55, when a CMU player stole the ball from guard Terry Donnelly and went in for a lay-up. He missed. The Spartans pulled down the rebound and got it to Jay Vincent, who went up for a basket, made it, and was fouled. He made the free throw and the three-point play. The game was over.

Earvin was pretty unhappy about his game. He had gotten better in the second half and had committed only one turnover. He wound up with seven points, nine rebounds, eight assists, four steals, and one blocked shot. It didn't add up to a bad game at all, but Earvin had expected to do much more, and he knew that much more had been expected of him. "I was scared," he later admitted. "Early in the game when I went up to shoot I didn't want to shoot. I had cramps in my stomach. But when we needed a pass for a basket I thought I played well under the pressure. I'll get better. I feel bad because of the way I played but I feel good because we won."

As for Coach Heathcote, he wondered what had happened to his promising team. Sure, they had won, but they had been poor on defense and poor in shooting and, what's more, they had allowed CMU to control the tempo of the game. The only thing that had saved them was that CMU had played as poorly as they had. "It was basketball at its worst," he said with a sigh.

Four days later the Spartans were in Syracuse, New York, for a college tournament called the Carrier Classic. After beating the University of Rhode Island, they went on to play Syracuse University for the tournament championship. The two teams were very well matched and the score was close all the way. Tied at 63-all with one minute to go, the squeaker was won by Syracuse. But the Spartans did not really mind. They knew that a team almost never wins a tight game on the road. They had played well, which added to their self-confidence. As Earvin said, "After the Syracuse game, I knew we could play anybody." Although his team lost, Earvin was named most valuable player of the tournament, which helped to make up for the loss to Syracuse, as well as his personal loss to CMU.

Back in East Lansing, the team had a five-day layoff before they met Witchita State at home. They used the time to practice hard. They had played three games together now, were getting used to one another, knew their weaknesses, and knew better what to work on in practice.

On the night of December 8th they showed how much they had improved. The Witchita Shockers were shocked themselves, 84-57. The gap in the score would have been even wider if the Spartans had not slowed down in the second half because they had such a big lead. When the final buzzer sounded, the Spartans knew they had played their best game so far. Bob Chapman had 15 points. Jay Vincent, who started at center, had 14. Greg Kelser had 11 rebounds. And Earvin Johnson, in his second game in the second sold-out at-home game of the season, really lived up to his nickname. He scored 19 points and had nine assists. His 20 rebounds were just nine short of the MSU all-time record. Several times in the course of the game, the crowd gave Earvin a standing ovation.

They did it for his passing and pretty shots, but his real skills were not the kind that the average fan notices. In rebounding, Earvin is not an exceptional jumper, but he seems to have a sixth sense about how the ball is going to fall. He is especially good at knowing where his own shots will bounce and many of his rebounds are the result of his following his own missed shots. Some of his passes were so quick that the fans missed them entirely. He turned the ball over eight times, but anyone who handled the ball as much as he did was bound to lose it from time to time.

The Spartans kept on winning. Two days later they beat Western Michigan 79-57. The following week they routed Middle Tennessee State 72-51. On December 21st they overpowered the University of Detroit 103-74. Looking back on the first part of the season, the Spartans and their coach were understandably pleased with their 6-1 record.

Each of the five starters was pleased because each had been given a chance to star in at least one game. Jay Vincent's moment of glory had come in the first game, Greg Kelser's against Western Michigan, and Terry Donnelly's against Middle Tennessee. Bob Chapman had played a couple of excellent games, and, of course, so had Earvin Johnson.

Earvin was the crowd pleaser, delighting the fans with his hand-slapping and broad grins each time one of his teammates made a basket or some other fine play. Always so "up," since that first game when he had suffered a severe case of the jitters, he had thrived on the roar of the crowd and the pressure to do well. The game in Detroit had been televised, and it had really been an exciting night for him: "TV, the crowd, it gets me fired up. It almost makes me want to dance a little." He was the sportswriters' dream, the kind of player who inspired them to clever writing, like calling him "the Spartans' exceptional freshman forward-center-guard-cheerleader-assistant coach." It was Earvin's picture that usually made the front pages of the sports sections of state and local papers after each game. Sometimes, when an article was supposed to be about Greg Kelser, the reporter wound up writing about Earvin Johnson.

After about five games, Earvin decided he'd better talk to his teammates about all the publicity. He explained that he didn't have any control over the press, and it was bothering him that he was getting most of the attention. Greg Kelser told reporters, "I understand that Earvin has supertalent and has a big local following. It doesn't matter who gets the headlines as long as we win. I don't have to do as much because we have tremendous balance, and that is what is going to give us a successful season. All I know is that we were 1-4 at this time last year without Earvin and we're 4-1 this season with him. But I really have to keep my eye on Earvin because some of his great passes make me look silly [if I'm not expecting them]."

Instead of becoming rivals, Earvin and Greg became close friends. They spent much of their off-court time together. Greg would eat at the Johnson home and Earvin went home to Detroit with Greg sometimes. Their fathers often telephoned each other to talk about basketball and their sons' progress. In the spring the two athletes joined a softball team—Greg was the 6-7 pitcher and Earvin the 6-8 third baseman. "Greg is like a brother to me," said Earvin.

Coach Heathcote could take some credit for his players' attitude. Over and over again, he tried to impress on them that it didn't matter who got the points or the glory as long as the team won. So far, the team had been winning and there had been no major personality problems among the players. But Heathcote realized all that could change if they started to lose. The coach knew that losing would bring jealousy to the surface—jealousy and bickering about playing time and who was to blame for each loss. He did not expect his team to start losing. But, he also realized they had yet to play another Big Ten team, and that the Spartans had some serious weaknesses which might show up in the face of stiff competition.

One of the team's major weaknesses was a lack of bench strength. The five starters played well together, but the reserves were not as skilled and did not get much playing time to develop what skill they did have. Heathcote realized that if one of his starters was injured, he had no one on the bench to step in. There wasn't much he could do, except hope his top five stayed healthy.

Another major weakness was defense. None of the starters was very strong in that area, except for rebounding. There are two basic types of defense in college basketball—the zone and the man-to-man. In the zone defense, each player defends an area in the opponents' end of the court and guards whatever opponents enter that area. In the man-to-man type of defense, each player is assigned to guard a particular opponent, but he must be able to switch off and help guard someone else when necessary. The Spartans had not been very good at the man-to-man defense. As Heathcote explained with a sigh, "We've got too many young kids who don't understand anything but checking your own man. And we haven't played [man-to-man] enough in games and that's my fault."

He had tried this kind of defense time and again, but had to switch quickly to the zone, with which his players had less trouble. The zone defense had drawbacks: it slowed down a game and made the fast break (getting the rebound and breaking fast for the other end of the court) difficult. Heathcote wished there was more time to practice different defensive patterns and more time to experiment in games, but he couldn't seem to find it. He just hoped the zone would work in the upcoming Big Ten contests.

After final exams, most MSU students went home for Christmas break, but the basketball team only had a short vacation. They had to practice for the Old Dominion Classic, to be held December 29th and 30th in Norfolk, Virginia. The Spartans won their first game in this tournament against Southern Methodist University easily, 95-69. Advancing to the finals, the Spartans routed the New Hampshire Wildcats 102-65 to capture the title. Earvin hit 10 of 12 shots from the field for 20 points and for the second time that season, was named most valuable player of a tournament. Soon after he got back to MSU he found out that he had not just passed his finals but had completed his first college semester with a solid B average.

If all this was not enough, Earvin also learned that he was the subject of some interest in the NBA. His coach and his family started getting calls, the most insistent ones from representatives of the Detroit Pistons. They wanted Earvin to leave college and turn pro at the end of the year. Earvin's parents didn't want

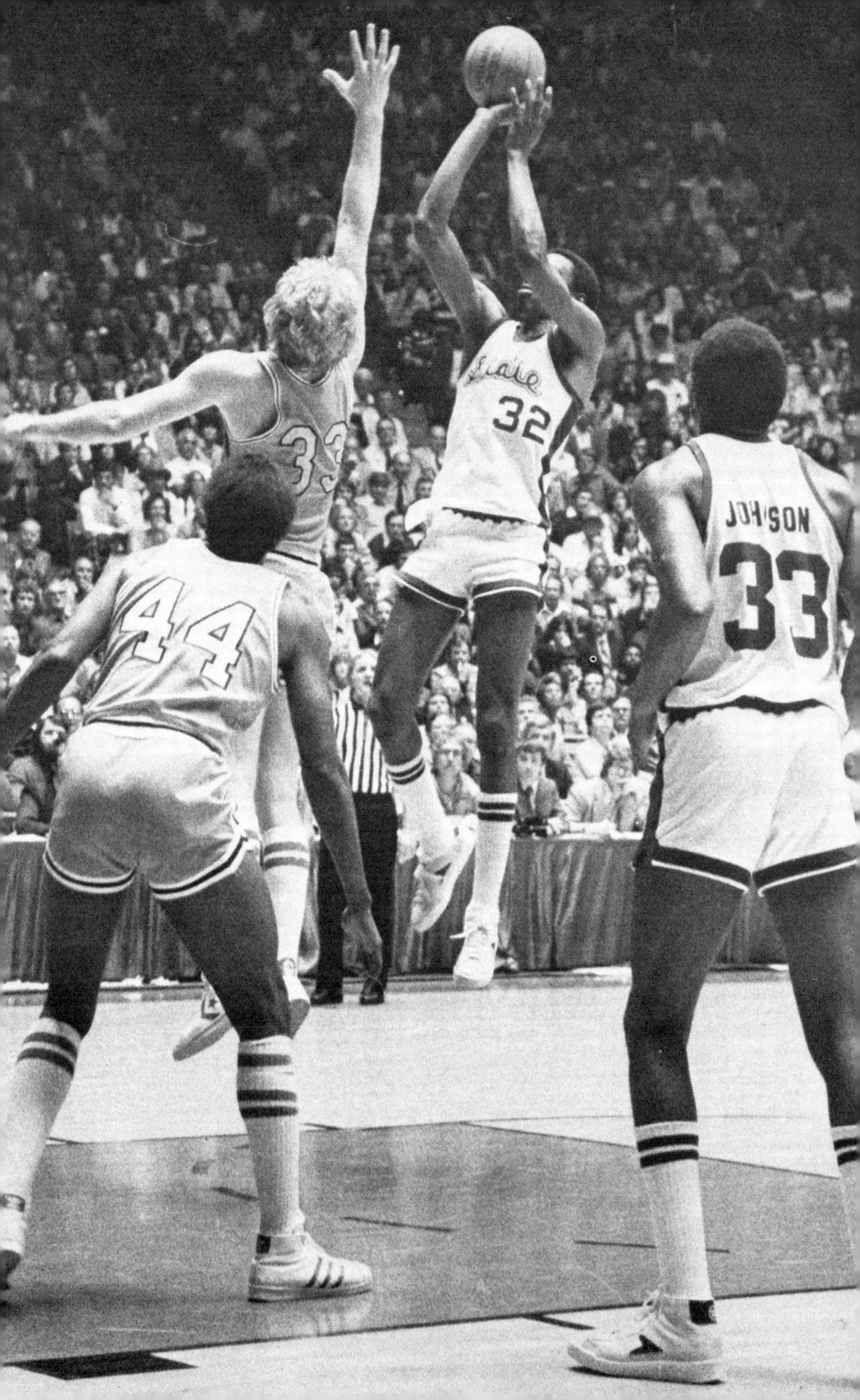

State
32
33
44
JOHNSON
33

their son's first year of college to be disrupted, and they certainly did not want more pressures on him during basketball season. Mr. Johnson and Dr. Tucker agreed to meet with the pro representatives and hear what they had to say but refused to make any decisions until the late spring.

Still, word got around quickly, and before long a lot of people were trying to guess whether Earvin would turn pro. When he was asked about it, he tried to shrug it off, but it was an issue that would come up more and more often as his freshman year wore on.

The Spartans met their first Big Ten rival in January 1978. The Big Ten is a conference in college athletics that is made up of ten colleges in the Middle West. These colleges aren't really any bigger than a lot of other colleges elsewhere, despite their name. The Big Ten teams compete against each other in all sports. Every year in every sport each college plays each of the others twice—once at home and once away. Winning the conference title is the highest glory one of these teams can achieve, short of winning a national title.

The Minnesota Gophers came to East Lansing for the first Big Ten contest with the Spartans. In the opening minutes of the game it looked as if the Spartans were going to blow the Gophers right back home. They outshot Minnesota by 17-2, and MSU quickly built up a 14-point lead. But Minnesota was an experienced team. They came back in the second half, hitting 20 of their first 31 shots, making the Spartan's zone defense, as Heathcote put it, "look like a sieve." Meanwhile, the Gophers switched their defense from a zone to a man-to-man strategy, forcing Greg Kelser into early foul trouble.

All eyes are on Greg Kelser and Larry Bird in the 1979 NCAA championship game. *Michigan State University*

But the Minnesota defensive switch helped Earvin Johnson. He had scored only six points in the first half. Going man-to-man, the Gophers put shorter, quicker men on him, and he suddenly found that his height advantage gave him a clearer shooting field. He had to use that advantage very quickly. With 2 1/2 minutes left to play, the Spartans were still down by seven points. Earvin happened to run past the Spartans' bench about then. Heathcote was wringing his hands in dismay. "Earvin, don't let the team lose," he pleaded. "We're not going to lose, coach," Earvin answered with a grin.

"Somehow," Heathcote recalls, "he just kind of pulled it out and we won by four." Magic became a "shooting machine," hitting long jumpers, twisting lay-ups, a great hook shot, and 13 of 15 foul shots. He scored 25 points in that second half and had a career-high game total of 31 points, plus eight rebounds and four assists. He was actually surprised to find out that he had scored so many points.

Meanwhile, Jay Vincent was doing his part, too. He had 22 points and seven assists, and after Greg Kelser fouled out with 6:22 left to go, he was an outstanding team player. Several of his assists came after Kelser left the game. It was this teamwork that made up for the weaknesses of the Spartans. When Earvin got back from the game that night, he said to his roommate, "Man, I think we can do it. I think we can win the Big Ten."

Chapter 5

By the end of January 1978, after wins over two other Big Ten schools, Iowa and Ohio State, the Michigan State University Spartans were ranked Number 7 in the nation. They were also one of the nation's top shooting teams, with a 55 percent field-goal shooting percentage. The win over Ohio State, the Spartans' thirteenth straight win, broke a school record. The Spartans were walking on air, and so was the entire student body, not to mention a majority of the population of Lansing-East Lansing.

But Jud Heathcote was a natural worrier. He worried even when there was nothing to worry about. Now, in the winter of 1978-79, he had good cause. So far, his team had managed to shoot well enough to overcome its defensive weaknesses, but there was still the lack of bench strength. In the game against Iowa he had sent freshman guard Mike Brkovich in for Bob Chapman when there were about ten minutes left to play. Almost immediately, Brkovich made three straight 20-foot jumpers. It reminded the coach that he had not developed the potential strength of his bench. Mike Brkovich had not played much at all, and perhaps he should have. On January 30, 1978,

Heathcote's worries proved well-founded. The Spartans' bubble burst. The University of Indiana upset them 71-66, halting their winning streak at the record-breaking 13 straight.

The Spartans did not enter the game under the best circumstances. For one thing, they had not been home in a week. They had left East Lansing on Wednesday to travel to Columbus for the Ohio State game. A blizzard struck and no one could get to the Ohio State field house. The team settled in at the Holiday Inn in Columbus and tried to make the best of things, but the blizzard made it necessary to reschedule a lot of games. The Spartans finally played Ohio State on Saturday instead of Thursday. This meant that their game against Indiana, originally scheduled for Saturday, had to be played on Monday.

By Monday they were tired. The hotel in Bloomington may have been a change of scene from the Holiday Inn in Columbus but it was still not home. Traveling through the snow had been slow and exhausting. The players' tempers were short, and their play showed it. They committed so many fouls that early in the game they found themselves in serious foul trouble. In fact, they had never before been in so much foul trouble. Greg Kelser, who usually fouled out a lot, ordinarily did so late in the game. This time, he fouled out after only 22 minutes with only eight points to his credit. Vincent and Chapman got into foul trouble, too. In fact, of the five starters, only Earvin Johnson played the whole 40 minutes. He led MSU with 21 points and 12 rebounds, but even his shooting was off—he hit only eight of 22 floor shots. The reserve players came in and did their best. In fact, without their efforts the scoring gap probably would have been much wider than it was at the end. The Hoosiers won, 71-66. A reason—just as Heathcote anticipated—was the Spartans' lack of bench strength.

Two nights later, the Spartans lost again—this time to the

University of Michigan, the defending Big Ten champions. This time the problem wasn't foul trouble as much as it was plain tiredness. It was the third game for the Spartans in six days, and they still hadn't recovered from the strain of being snowbound and having two of their games rescheduled. Of course, Michigan had suffered the same predicament. The difference between the two teams, once again, was bench strength.

When the Indiana Hoosiers roared into town three nights later, it looked as if that two-game losing streak might grow to a three-game losing streak. Jay Vincent was out with the flu. Substitute center Jim Coutre had three fouls before the game was three minutes old. Ron Charles replaced Coutre, and 11 minutes later he, too, had three fouls. Stan Feldretch, who was averaging only six minutes playing time per game, then became the Spartans' center. And, the team was not shooting well—only 40 percent from the floor and just four of 15 from the free-throw line. At the half they were lucky to be trailing by only five points.

Three minutes into the second half, the Spartans were down by 11 points, 45-34. It was hardly the time to start experimenting with his team's known weak points, but Coach Heathcote didn't know what else to do. He left Feldretch, Johnson, and Kelser in. Mike Brkovich was sent in to play guard, and Ron Charles, with three fouls, to play forward. When the score was 48-42, Heathcote also ordered his team to switch from a zone to a man-to-man defense.

There they were—two regulars playing their usual positions, one regular guard playing forward, and two reserves (who had not known much playing time) trying to execute a defensive strategy at which they were not very good. But the changes worked, and they proved to be the turning point of the game. MSU took control. Keeping Indiana scoreless, the team reeled off a string of six points. Brkovich hit two 19-foot jumpers and Charles stuffed one on an assist from Johnson. Suddenly, the score was tied at 48-all. The Hoosiers scored a field goal at last, but MSU followed with eight straight points, and they never led by less than four points again. The Spartans won the game 68-59, and the tenth straight sellout crowd at Jenison Field House went wild.

Down on the court, when the final buzzer sounded, the Spartans went wild, too. They knew just how important this victory was. It was not just that three losses in a row would have been awfully hard to take but, equally important, just about everyone on the team had contributed. For these young men and their coach the teamwork made it their best victory so far. The newspapers might give credit for the win to the "scoring and rebounding of junior Greg Kelser and the all-round excellence of Earvin Johnson," but the Spartans themselves gave credit to the Spartans—every single one of them.

A few days later, the team avenged their loss to the University of Michigan by beating the Wolverines 73-62 on their home court. It was the first time MSU had beaten U.M. since 1973, and only the sixth time that the Wolverines had lost in their home court in 66 games. The Wolverines' coach had high praise for the Spartan team, especially for Earvin Johnson. He told a reporter for the *Detroit Free Press*, "Johnson plays forward, guard, center and even coaches a little, too. And he doesn't do a bad job. The [Detroit] Pistons would be smart to draft him. He'd fill that Silverdome in Pontiac. They're throwing all that money around to people who can't play. They might as well give it to a player. He's a great player. I'd like to see him turn pro."

Although Earvin, who had scored 25 points, had eight rebounds and six assists, brightened when he heard about the rival coach's praise, he quickly turned serious when a *Detroit News* reporter brought up turning pro. "I don't want to get saying that now," he said, stumbling over his words a little. "I don't want to say anything to affect the other players. So I'm going to play hard and wait until the end of the season and see."

Of course he was thinking about turning pro; he couldn't help it. He loved the game of basketball, and he was showing he was good at it. Naturally, he couldn't help being affected by the attention and the praise. At the same time, he realized that all this speculation about his turning pro was disrupting not just his life but the life of his team. The last thing he wanted to do was get his teammates upset.

At such times, he would talk with his parents who told him very simply and clearly that it was not the time to think about anything but college and college basketball. After a good home-cooked meal, while his brothers and sisters brought him up to date on what they were doing, he would feel like "plain old Earvin" again.

The Spartans continued to win. On February 23rd they beat Northwestern 66-56 for their twentieth season win. It was the first time an MSU team had won that many games in one season in *79 years* of basketball. Now that Heathcote was going to his bench more often, the Spartans' reserves were getting more practice at staying alert to Earvin's lightning-quick passes. (Like Greg Kelser and the other starters, they were finding out how silly they looked when the ball bounced off their unsuspecting heads.) The team was also getting better at switching from the zone to the man-to-man defense to pick up the pace of a game.

By the end of February, the Spartans seemed to have staked out a claim at least to a tie for the Big Ten championship.

Coach Heathcote had not really expected they would get that far when the season started. His goal was to get to the National Collegiate Athletic Association (NCAA) tournament. "The tournament berth was our Number 1 objective," he said after the Spartans beat Illinois and clinched the Big Ten title, "but now we've achieved at least our Number 2 goal with the Big Ten championship. As long as we're in this situation, with a piece of the title, we may as well go out and win it outright."

All the colleges in the country belong to the NCAA. It sets the rules, draws up the schedules, and keeps statistics on almost all intercollegiate sports. At the end of each sport's season, the NCAA sponsors a tournament that pits the best teams in the nation against each other. Only in the NCAA tournament could the Spartans see how they matched up against other best teams in the country—teams that were not on their regular season or other special tournament schedules.

By beating Wisconsin and Minnesota in their two remaining regular-season games, the Spartans finished the season having achieved both their goals—the Big Ten championship and a chance to play in the NCAA tournament. For Earvin Johnson the regular season ended with his having placed first in the league in assists, tied for third in scoring, fifth in free-throw percentage, and tied for sixth in rebounding. Not only was he a unanimous All-Big Ten team selection, he was the only freshman named to an All-America team. He was also the only freshman selected to play for the U.S. college team that would play Cuba, Yugoslavia, and the USSR later that spring.

Unfortunately, Coach Heathcote's worst fears were realized

Johnson demonstrates the classic dribble. *Michigan State University*

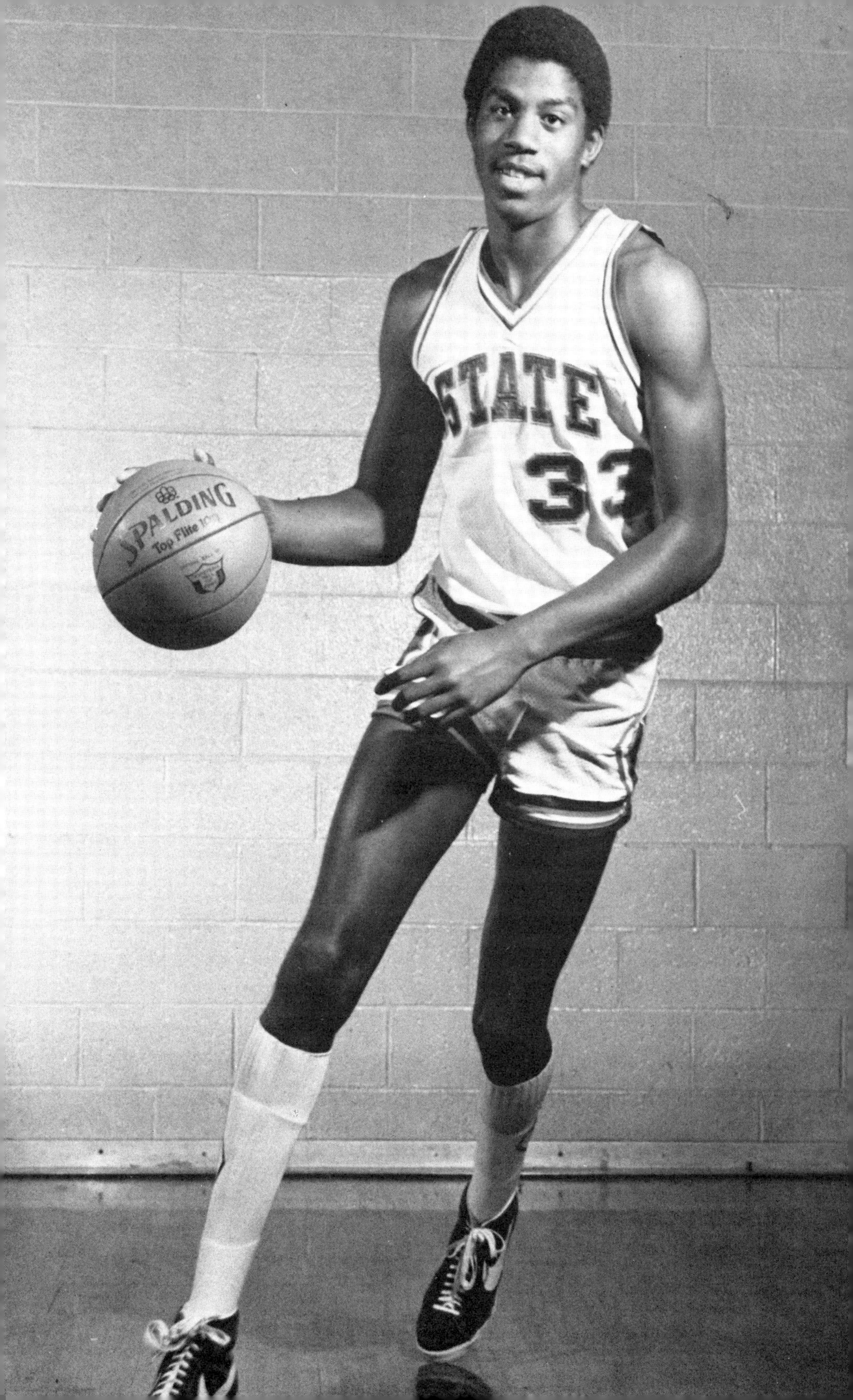
STATE
33
SPALDING
Top Flite 100

within a week after the close of the regular season. A series of injuries and illnesses struck the Spartans. Four days after the final game of the regular season, Earvin Johnson and Jay Vincent collided in practice and each of them injured a foot. The next day they were both hobbling around on crutches. They tried to make a joke of it, although they knew that any injuries at this time were a serious matter. The next blow came when reserve center Jim Coutre announced that he wasn't feeling well. It turned out that he had mononucleosis.

Coutre was the only Spartan who stayed behind in East Lansing when the rest of the team set off for Indianapolis, Indiana, where the first tournament game was to be played. Both Earvin and Jay were judged well enough to go, and they waved to the huge crowd that had gathered to see them off. "Go Spartans!" and "Bring Back the Championship!" signs waved in the cold March air as the university band played the MSU song. The two freshman looked at each other and grinned: who would have guessed that they would get to the NCAA their first year in college?

It was obvious that Earvin was feeling better because when he arrived at the team's hotel in Indianapolis, he managed to carry both his luggage and a large portable radio. He bopped along, dancing to the tune. There was nothing wrong with his foot now. He knew the coach was worried because he and Jay had missed two days of practice but, after all, they had been practicing and playing all season.

At practice in Indianapolis' Market Square Arena on Saturday, starting guard Terry Donnelly took a knee in the upper right thigh. Later, Bob Chapman came down on his ankle the wrong way. "Jeez," Coach Heathcote complained, "Can't we hold a practice without somebody getting hurt!" Luckily, the injuries were minor. All four injured starters were in the lineup the next night and, if they were not at the top of their form, they were still very determined to win. As the Providence College coach joked, "From what I hear about Earvin he can probably play on crutches better than most guys can on two legs."

Providence College was MSU's first NCAA opponent, and the Rhode Island team had a lot more experience than the Spartans. There were four seniors and a junior on the team, and they had played in two previous NCAA tournaments as well as a National Invitational Tournament. All that experience did not count for much when they went up against the Spartans, who may have been young and inexperienced but made up for that in determination.

Earvin decided to favor his ankle and took only three shots in the first 34 minutes of play. His style of shooting—shooting on the run, off balance—could really make the injury worse. "They didn't need me to shoot," he said later. "My players took over. Hey, we're an explosive team."

My players? That's how Earvin thought of his teammates, and that's why sportswriters often referred to him as a sort of unofficial assistant coach. If Coach Heathcote ever objected, he didn't do so publicly. Earvin was so enthusiastic that it was hard to dampen his spirit. At any rate, the Spartans, whomever they belonged to, did indeed take over. They shot an amazing 64 percent from the field and took almost all the important rebounds. By halftime the score was 38-26. Within the first five minutes of the second half the Spartans reeled off ten straight points to take a 20-point lead. Providence rallied and cut the lead to 12 points, but then Earvin took over. He scored nine straight points and led an 18-8 burst that brought the Spartan lead back to 24 points. Providence cut ten points off that lead, but still lost by 14 in the end.

Magic did not score a lot of points in that game, but as Coach Heathcote said afterward, "That was Earvin's ordinary game you saw out there today. Remember, he led the Big Ten in assists [with an amazing 269]. When it comes to putting the ball in the basket he can do that, too."

The NCAA quarter finals were next for the Spartans. The team set off for Dayton, Ohio, to play Western Kentucky, which had beaten Syracuse, the team that had handed MSU its first loss in the Carrier Classic back in early December 1977. Once again, Earvin did not score much. This was partly because Western Kentucky had three or four men guarding him every time he got the ball near the basket. He made only three of 17 from the field, but he handed out a season-high 14 assists. The Spartans won the game 90-69, but Coach Heathcote was not all that pleased with the rout. He had seen a trend in the game that he did not like. The Spartans had been lousy at controlling their own defensive boards.

Now Kentucky, which was ranked Number 1 in the nation, was the only team standing between the Spartans and the NCAA finals. The game was played in Dayton on Saturday, March 18th.

The game began like earlier tournament games. The Spartans took an early lead, and by halftime they were ahead 27-22. As in the earlier games, Earvin Johnson was not doing much scoring. Kentucky was using a one-three-one zone defense against him and was effectively cutting him off from the ball on offense. The zone also forced him into foul trouble, which did not usually happen.

Midway into the second half, several of the Spartans were in foul trouble, and they had to play cautiously. Coach Heathcote chose not to go to his bench very much in this game where so much was at stake. With six minutes and 16 seconds left in the game, the score was 41-all, but then Kentucky made a three-point play and MSU guards Bob Chapman and Terry Donnelly fouled out. Still, the Spartans were trailing by only one point with 23 seconds left to play.

Mike Brkovich committed a foul with eight seconds to go and the Kentucky player on the line made both free throws. As time ran out, Earvin tried a desperate 35-foot shot. It fell short. As the buzzer sounded, the Spartans faced an experience they had not had often over the past four months—losing. This experience was even worse because they had not just lost a game but their one and only chance to go on to the NCAA finals.

Earvin was devastated. Although he had been named to the all-tournament team, along with Greg Kelser, he took personal blame for the loss. He stood before a crowd of newsmen in the mass interview room at the University of Dayton and said so: "My whole tournament was bad. I don't know any reason for it. I just tried to do other things when my shots wouldn't fall."

His teammates, notably Greg Kelser, thought Earvin was being too hard on himself. "I don't agree with Earvin," said Greg. "Maybe his shots didn't fall but he did other things for us." But try telling that to a young man who refers to his teammates as "my players." Earvin always considered himself the leader of the team, and it followed that he was to blame if the team lost. He was not a crybaby about it, but it rankled the rest of the team a bit. It seemed to them that if you were going to "talk team" in win situations, you ought to do the same when you lose. Earvin was being a little bit uppity about all this, and it was not the first time. Some of the other players' resentment about all the glory Earvin received came out now that they had lost. It was a natural reaction. But they didn't put Earvin Johnson down, they simply voted Greg Kelser the team's most valuable player.

Although Earvin was pleased for his teammate and partner in

the pass-and-dunk play that the two did so well, he realized that his teammates had some reservations about him. Try as he might, he could not help being bothered by it. If the attitude of his teammates had any bearing on the question of his turning pro at the end of that year, Earvin has never said. The deadline for filing for the NBA draft as a hardship case was April 25th. "There is never any time to decide," Earvin complained.

Actually, he'd had quite a bit of time, but he had put off serious consideration of turning pro until the basketball season was over. Now, it was over, and the decision had to be made. The next two weeks were not going to be easy.

Earvin clammed up to reporters for the next two weeks, or at least he tried to. But there were calls--hundreds and hundreds of calls—from reporters, from fans, from friends. Those who expressed an opinion were almost evenly divided for and against his turning pro. Earvin himself wanted very much to join the NBA. "I really wanted to go hardship," he said after it was all over. "It wasn't so much the fact of all that money as it was finally realizing the dream of being a professional that I've had so long."

But there were other, more powerful people involved in the decision-making process—his parents. Mrs. Johnson thought her son was a superb basketball player who would have no trouble in the pros. She did not worry much about his age or the level of his maturity. But she did worry about his education. She wanted him to have a college degree and, in her opinion, since he had started college, he ought to finish.

Magic flashes his famous smile as he poses with his All-American Basketball Team trophy. *Michigan State University*

The Sporting News
Presents This Certificate to
EARVIN JOHNSON
Michigan State University
In Recognition of His Selection to
The Sporting News
1978-79 All-America Basketball Team
C. C. JOHNSON SPINK
Chairman
MICHIGAN
33
STATE

Earvin Johnson, Sr., was not so concerned with the degree. The boy was only 18, which meant that he could certainly find time to get his degree in the next few years, even if his education was interrupted by pro ball. What concerned Mr. Johnson was that his son might go pro before he was ready, and for an insufficient amount of money to boot. He and Dr. Tucker were very careful to talk about such things to the pro representatives who besieged Earvin Johnson that spring.

No one published the exact figures, but rumor had it that one team had offered him $1.5 million. Later, it was revealed that the Kansas City Kings had offered him $250,000 a year for six years. All Earvin knew was that the whole thing was complicated, and full of pressure. "There was a lot of dealing going on at the end," he said later. "I was hoping to the end that something might break and I'd get a chance to turn pro."

Earvin Johnson, Sr., decided that the money being offered was not worth his son's giving up a second year of experience in college basketball. And, in the end, although the final decision was up to Earvin, he went along with his father. "It was the hardest decision I've ever had to make in my life," he told a *Detroit News* sportswriter in late April. "Choosing a college was small stuff compared to what I've been going through the last couple of weeks. The decision concerns my future, my life, and they were talking a lot of money."

Earvin buried his regrets by playing basketball, and he had a variety of basketball experiences that spring and summer, in a variety of places. As a second team All-American selection, he went to Europe with the U.S. college team. Traveling to different countries was fun, although he did not get to do much besides play basketball. He also enjoyed the experience of playing under international rules, which differed from the rules of basketball to which he was accustomed. His team went all the way to the finals before losing to the Soviet Union.

Somehow, he also managed to squeeze in a visit to some relatives in North Carolina that summer, and to show some people in the town of Rocky Mount that he wasn't called "Magic" for nothing. Hearing that Earvin was in town, a local basketball star challenged him to a one-on-one match. Whoever could make 15 baskets first would win. The stakes were $20 apiece. Earvin accepted the challenge. It looked at first as if the Rocky Mount player was going to win easily. He ran off six straight baskets without Earvin's scoring at all, but he never made another basket because the next 15 were Earvin's. The local hero was embarrassed. He tried to get his friends to lend him more money so he could play Earvin again, but they wouldn't do it. Nobody in Rocky Mount, North Carolina, was going to bet against the Magic Man.

Chapter 6

Earvin Johnson's second year of college began in a rather unique way. *Sports Illustrated* magazine wanted to do a cover story about the "classiness" of college basketball for one of its fall issues. As one of the outstanding college players in the nation, Earvin was asked to pose for the cover photograph. Dressed up in a tuxedo, complete with top hat and patent leather shoes, he was photographed taking shots on a basketball court. He also posed with other top college sophomores, all in tuxedos, in a formal parlor setting.

The story, which appeared in the November 27, 1978, issue, featured Magic on the cover, leaping in midair, tipping in a behind-the-back, left-handed lay-up, and flashing his famous grin. Inside, the major article on college basketball was devoted to him. Not surprisingly, it created quite a stir on the MSU campus. "Everybody was bringing magazines to class for me to autograph," Magic recalls, "and the profs held up class and let me get all that out of the way."

Otherwise, his professors did not treat him any differently from the other students. They behaved toward him as they had when he was a freshman. He was expected to be prepared for his classes and to get his assignments in on time. This term he was taking social science, humanities, and some communications courses—16 credit hours altogether, even though basketball season would begin during the term. "I definitely have to budget time for studying," he said,"—three or four hours every evening to try to get it all done."

He could have taken fewer courses, but he did not want to get behind. If he decided to turn pro at the end of his sophomore year, he wanted to have completed the number of credits necessary to be a full-fledged junior when he did return.

On top of his regular courses, he was still taking the special reading course over at the Learning Resources Center. "It's really improved my speed-reading," he said. "I'm up to about 500 words a minute now . . . I was down, like to maybe 200." Not only had the center done a lot for Earvin, he had done a lot for it in return. Before he had signed up for the course, many people on the MSU campus had considered the center as a place for "lost causes." The general opinion was that only dumb students went there. Of course, that was not true at all. The center was a place for improving skills. Athletes, with their grueling practice and game schedules, often did not have the time to do all their reading for class. The courses at the center took extra time, but they taught the athletes to read and understand what they were reading more quickly.

Earvin Johnson understood how much the reading course could help him. He was not afraid the other students would think him "dumb." His attitude gave the center "respectability." Now, other students—athletes and nonathletes—were taking the center's courses and improving their skills, too.

Earvin was concentrating fully on college now. The decision to turn pro or not was months away. In the meantime, he was putting it out of his mind. "I can't be in there half-stepping—

halfway going pro and halfway in college," he said. "I'm all the way in college now and I have to treat it like that." The only major change he made was to move out of the dorm and into an off-campus apartment with Andy Wells, who was on the track team. Earvin had decided he could concentrate on his studies better in that environment.

Before long he was all the way into college basketball again, too. There was little question that the Spartans were the team to beat this year. Five of the top six players on the last year's team were back. In fact, Coach Heathcote liked to say that the team could win the NCAA championship if the rules were changed and a team could be limited to just five men. The coach believed that senior Greg Kelser, juniors Terry Donnelly and Ron Charles, and sophomores Earvin Johnson and Jay Vincent could take on the top five players of any other team. But MSU's bench—mostly freshmen and sophomores who had not had much playing experience—was still weak. The team also had lost its best outside shooter with the graduation of Bob Chapman. Still, the team was ranked seventh in the Associated Press preseason poll. In addition, it got a head start on the season by going on a tour to Brazil, playing basketball teams in several cities there. In Coach Heathcote's opinion, if the team could stay free of injuries, they would go all the way this year. He confided to Larry Keith of *Sports Illustrated*, "I tell the players it takes five things for us to win. In order, they are teamwork, the fast break, defense, field-goal shooting, and offense. I let Earvin take care of the first two, and I handle the rest."

Earvin was named co-captain of the team mainly because Coach Heathcote was pretty sure this would be his last season at MSU. He wasted no time taking charge. In preparation for the very first game, Earvin added to his list of activities (guard-forward-cheerleader-assistant coach) the role of scout. The Spartans' first opponents that season were the Soviet national team. Earvin had played against them in Europe earlier that year, and he told his coach and his teammates what to expect from a team that included two seven-foot-tall players and two others who were six-foot ten inches in height. "I knew them and it made a lot of difference," he said after the game. "I knew they would take the ball up and then bring it down low before they took a shot, and that got us a lot of steals." The Spartans beat the Russians 76-60. Earvin had 13 assists and five steals, one of them from a seven-foot player. To be fair, the Russians, who had won six of their first seven games in the United States, had an exhausting schedule and were showing the effects of it by the time they got to East Lansing. But Earvin didn't care why his team won: "I like to win, period. If we're playing the Russians, street ball, or just messing around."

For the next month or so, Earvin and his teammates did win. They beat Central Michigan, Cal State-Fullerton, and Western Michigan in nonconference games. Even so, the Spartans were not really playing good basketball. There would be moments of brilliance, but there were also times when, as Heathcote put it, "we looked like a YMCA team." When the Spartans lost to North Carolina in a squeaker, 70-69, it didn't seem to perk them up. Although they won their next game against Cincinnati, they were still not playing with much enthusiasm or intensity. As a matter of fact, Heathcote got so angry at Kelser and Johnson that he benched them both in the last five minutes of the first half.

The Spartans realized they were not playing the way they had the year before, but nobody was sure why they weren't. Maybe the reason was simple. Perhaps they were tired and needed a break. They got one in mid-December because of final exams.

Magic goes high for a lay-up during the 1979 NCAA championship game against Indiana State. *Wide World Photos*

There was pressure at that time, too, but at least it was a different kind of pressure.

By the end of the first week in January, having beaten both Wisconsin and Minnesota, the Spartans were ranked first in the Big Ten. The next two games on the conference schedule were away and involved traveling in terrible weather. It was an especially hard winter, and there were many delays and postponed games. When they reached Champaign to play Illinois, they were exhausted.

Illinois was ranked Number 4 in the Big Ten standings, but that ranking did not do justice to their play. They had won 14 games in a row, and in the eyes of their fans at least, they were Number 1. Needless to say, bad weather or not, everyone—including the governor of Illinois—wanted to see the Illini play the first-ranked team. The crowd of 16,209 was the largest in the 16-year history of Assembly Hall.

The Spartans came out strong, hitting 11 of their first 12 shots from the field. But the Illini ran off a 21-6 streak in the second period and led by four at the half. The game was nip-and-tuck throughout the second half. There were five ties and many lead changes. The teams were never more than a couple of points apart. In the closing seconds, with the score tied, it looked as if the game would go into overtime. But with three seconds left, Eddie Johnson of Illinois sank an 18-foot jumper from the baseline, and the Spartans were left with that empty feeling of having come close to winning but not quite making it.

Two days later, against Purdue in West Lafayette, Indiana, the Spartans lost another game by a single basket that was made with only seconds remaining on the clock. The feeling of emptiness began to turn into despair, but few people were counting MSU out. There were still 15 games to go, all but two of them Big Ten conference games. Since eight of those games would be played at Jenison Field House, the Spartans still had a good chance to win the conference title.

After the Spartans lost four of six games in January, including one-point losses to Michigan and Northwestern, Coach Heathcote decided to make some changes. The major change was to move Earvin Johnson from guard to forward. Mike Brkovich came off the bench to play guard, and forward Ron Charles was retired to the bench as a substitute. After that, the Spartans started to win again.

George Fox, Earvin's high school coach, had been following the progress of the MSU team, and especially the progress of his former star. He thought Heathcote had made a good move. "It took Jud Heathcote a while to realize how good Earvin is at bringing the ball down the court," says Fox. "As a freshman, he was restricted in his basketball skills coming up the court; by his sophomore year he totally dominated the ball-handling."

Earvin had no trouble adjusting to his new role. He seemed to like the increased versatility the change from guard to forward allowed. And, he certainly liked winning again, as did his teammates. When the season ended, the Spartans had a 21 and six record. They were eligible to play in the NCAA tournament.

Many of the Spartans were aware that this would probably be their last chance to win the NCAA title. Greg Kelser was graduating, and Earvin Johnson would probably not be back. For this particular Spartan team, at any rate, it was now or never. Coach and players sat down and mapped out their goals. To go all the way, they would have to win five games. They decided to take the games one at a time, step-by-step, and to concentrate completely on each step in turn. They would play each game as if it were the final game, and maybe in that way they would not mess up their chances for the real final game, as they had the year before.

Chapter 7

Michigan State University was "seeded," or ranked, second to Notre Dame (which had a 22-5 record) in the NCAA Mideast region. Each drew a first-round "bye," which meant that they didn't have to play until the second round. In the second round, MSU would play the winner of a first-round contest between the University of Detroit and Lamar College in Texas. The Spartans expected Detroit to win, because it was a better team, and were surprised when Lamar took the game. They didn't think Lamar could manage two upset victories, and although Jay Vincent sprained his ankle in the first half, the Spartans trounced Lamar 95-64. Step 1 was complete.

Greg Kelser had 31 points in that game. Earvin Johnson had ten assists, most of them to Kelser. "It's going to make him money," said Earvin to a *Detroit News* reporter after the game. "We want to show the pro recruiters, or whatever they call them, what he can do. He's the senior, and you got to get your shot now. We want to help get him the fattest contract he can."

For Step 2, the Spartans met the Louisiana State University Tigers. The Tigers' pregame strategy was to take an early lead and then freeze the ball the rest of the game. Kelser and

Johnson foiled that strategy. Kelser sparked his team's effort with two intercepted passes, which he converted into driving dunks, and then Johnson really caught fire. His 24 points were contribution enough, but he also had 12 assists, many of them expert passes that set up more dunks for Kelser. The Spartans won the game 79-71, but they lost center Jay Vincent. Jay suffered a foot injury, and it could not have happened at a worse time. MSU still had no depth at all on its bench. Ron Charles would take Vincent's place, but he would need a great deal of help.

With Step 2 complete, MSU could concentrate on Notre Dame in the regional finals. The two teams had started the season as the area's highest ranked and each had spent some time as Number 1 in the nation. The biggest difference between them was depth. As Coach Heathcote put it, "Notre Dame goes at you with nine players, and we come back at you with two."

The two, of course, were Kelser and Johnson, who worked beautifully together on a play called the lob and dunk. Earvin would lob a pass to Kelser and Kelser would dunk the ball. The day before the Notre Dame game, Earvin teased Greg that he wasn't as good a dunker as UCLA's David Greenwood. Greg retorted that they would see about that the next day.

The game began with Kelser batting the opening tip to Johnson, who flipped the ball over his head to Mike Brkovich, breaking for the dunk. But Notre Dame followed with two points of its own, and the game was close for the first quarter. In the second period the difference between the two teams became evident. Notre Dame's coach, Digger Phelps, made a lot of lineup changes, and the same five players were never on the court together long enough to get any kind of rhythm going. By contrast, the same five MSU players were on court practically all the time. Midway in the second half, with

Magic passes in semifinal game of the 1979 NCAA championship against Penn State. *Wide World Photos*

Michigan ahead by three points, Earvin and Greg really began to connect. "A little eye contact is all we need," Greg said later. "I know what he's looking for and he knows what I'm looking for." The two made eye contact, and in a sudden spurt Greg scored seven straight baskets, four of them on passes from Earvin, to extend the lead from three to nine. Notre Dame didn't know what hit them.

The Irish never got closer than seven points after that. Greg and Magic pretty much controlled the game. The dunker wound up with 34 points, the passer with 13 assists. Jay Vincent's absence and the lack of bench strength had not hindered them at all, especially not Earvin.

Earvin had more than his usual desire to win behind his energetic play. He had a feeling that the Spartans would not be in the NCAA tournament the next year. Greg Kelser was a senior. And maybe he, Earvin, would be playing NBA basketball. There was a good chance that for both him and Greg it was "now or never."

The win over Notre Dame advanced the Spartans to the NCAA semifinals. In that tournament, the four remaining teams would play two contests on the same day in the University of Utah's Special Events Center. Top-ranked Indiana State would play second-ranked DePaul, and the third-ranked MSU Spartans would play the fourth-ranked Quakers of Penn State. The winners of the two contests would play each other for the championship.

MSU and Penn played first. It was the Quakers' first time ever in the semifinals and their playing seemed to be affected by stage fright. At one point a Penn player passed to a teammate who was standing out of bounds! In no time at all, the score was 38-8 in the Spartans' favor. At half time, it was 50-17—the widest first-half margin in the history of the NCAA semifinals. The contest was no contest, and the fans got bored. "We want the Bird," some of them began to chant.

They were calling for Larry Bird, the Indiana State star. A superb scorer, Bird was as famous as Earvin Johnson—more famous, perhaps—because he had led his team in an amazing 32-game winning streak and because, as a senior, he had been a star longer. Fans and reporters often compared the two players, although their styles of play were almost entirely different. The comparisons had become "either-or" contrasts: you could not like them both; you had to like one better than the other.

In early March, Joe Falls, a staff writer for the *Detroit News* wrote a headline article saying Bird was better than Johnson. He allowed that Bird was three years older and had had two years more experience than Johnson, but he rated the two on their performances in various aspects of the game. Bird—as the table shows—came out better in everything but "charisma."

	Bird	Johnson
Shooting	9	4
Passing	9	9
Rebounding	8	6
Floor sense	10	9
Charisma	8	10
Totals	44	38

A lot of people didn't agree with Falls, especially about the "charisma" rating for Bird, which they thought was much too high. Later that month *News* writer, Mike O'Hara, wrote, "This is Bird's fifth college year. If he is an example of the benefits of college, then Johnson could have turned pro after kindergarten. There is that much difference between these two brilliant players." Similar statements were in many of the nation's newspapers that spring.

Johnson and Bird—the objects of the controversy—hardly knew one another. Their schools did not play each other during the regular season. Their only experience on the court together had come the previous summer when both had been part of the U.S. All-Star team that had gone to Europe.

"I've been on the same floor with Bird," said Earvin. "We threw each other some nice passes. We got the crowd going. We had some fun. He's a good guy, great." And Bird said, "Earvin Johnson is probably one of the best players I ever played with." Neither of the two wanted to get caught up in the controversy but that was going to be hard.

Earvin Johnson did not like to hear the fans call for Larry Bird, but he didn't let this affect his play, any more than Greg Kelser did. Once again, the two combined for five baskets, two of them dunks. Magic wound up with 29 points, ten rebounds, and ten assists. Kelser had 28 points and nine rebounds. The Spartans' team as a whole matched two NCAA semifinals records, scoring 101 points and winning by 34.

In the game that followed, Indiana State beat DePaul by one point: 75-74. The stage was set for an exciting duel between Michigan State and Indiana, between Magic Johnson and Larry Bird. MSU guard Terry Donnelly told reporters that he was so excited about seeing the two play against one another that he wouldn't mind just sitting in the stands and watching. As it turned out, it was a good thing Donnelly was out on the court and not in the stands. The game was not a two-man confrontation. The whole Spartan team was exciting to watch.

Coach Heathcote took no chances in preparing for that championship game. His team had played very well in the last month, but that did not mean they could loaf before the all-important match. Although Heathcote was aware that Larry Bird always said Johnson was more of a passer and that he was more of a shooter, Bird was, in fact, a fine passer himself. Heathcote wanted to be sure his players were ready to head off those passes. In practice, he had Magic passing *against* his teammates. Earvin got right into the spirit and tried his best to impersonate Bird. "He had a good time throwing up 30-footers," said Heathcote. "That's what Bird does."

Heathcote also set up a special zone defense with Bird in mind, a matchup zone that put "a man-and-a-half" on the Indiana State star. That meant that one man would guard him and another man would come in to help out. Above all, Heathcote advised his players to "stay loose." "Don't tighten up because we're up against Bird and a team that has won 32 straight games," he said. "If you can play the way you've played the last month, you'll do it."

Earvin Johnson, for one, didn't need such advice. He was playing in the NCAA championship and planning to enjoy every minute of it. That was another important difference between Johnson and Bird. Before the game, the Indiana State star told *Sports Illustrated* reporter Larry Keith, "To me it's a very serious game. I can't be laughing like he does out there. I just hope when it's over he ain't laughing at me."

Five minutes into the game, Terry Donnelly took his first shot and put his team into the lead. The Spartans played brilliantly, doing what they had to do, they contained Larry Bird. The man-and-a-half defense worked very well—Bird's teammates could not get the ball to him. On the rare occasions when Bird did get the ball, he had no shot. If he tried to pass off to someone else, he had a hard time finding anyone open. Bird was thoroughly frustrated. He shot only seven for 21, scored only 19 points, had only two assists, and committed six turnovers. Meanwhile, at the other end of the court, the Spartans were putting on a show of teamwork with highly balanced scoring. Johnson led all Spartans with 24 points; Kelser had 19; but guard Terry Donnelly, after averaging only 6.3 points in earlier tournament games, had 15 points. The team also had balanced rebounding.

In the fading moments of the game, with victory assured, Magic and Greg put their arms around each other near midcourt. Said Greg later, "I just stopped, looked him in the eye and told him, 'you played one heck of a game.' He told me I was a bad dude, stuff I'd been hearing all year." Then they joined the rest of their teammates.

When the buzzer sounded, the Spartans had won the game 75-64. The new NCAA basketball champions jumped around on the floor, on each other, screaming, "We're Number 1!" Under the basket, Johnson and Kelser hugged each other. Then Earvin looked over at Indiana's bench where Bird sat, sobbing, his head buried in a towel. The grin of victory left Earvin's face. He knew how hard it was to lose. He had no desire whatsoever to laugh at Larry Bird. Bird's consolation was that he was named College Player of the Year, which grated on Johnson. After all, Bird's team had lost the NCAA finals, while his team had won. But Magic tried not to let it bother him. Winning the championship was the important thing. Before they left for home, one of the Spartans wrote on the bulletin board of the Special Events Center, "Step 5 Complete."

With the NCAA tournament over, college basketball was over for another season, but there was no letdown for Magic Johnson. All the Spartans were heroes to the school and the surrounding community, but Earvin was practically a legend. An East Lansing motel put on its marquee, "If you believe in Magic, welcome." Everywhere he went, he was besieged by autograph-seekers and people who just wanted to shake his hand. Strange girls called him at all hours of the day and night, and his roommate, Andy Wells, was getting a little jealous. A reporter from *Sports Illustrated* came to do a whole article just on him.

Johnson was hounded by reporters and Spartans' fans asking him what he was going to do. He had put off the decision for the duration of the season but it could not be put off much longer. He would have to declare hardship by May 11th to be eligible for the June 25th NBA draft.

In discussions with his family and Dr. Tucker, Earvin realized he had several options. 1. He could finish college and then turn pro. This would give him a degree in telecommunications and enable him to try out for the US 1980 Olympics basketball team. 2. He could return to MSU for his junior year, then announce his intention to turn pro and be drafted by an NBA team. He would probably still be eligible to play in the summer Olympics because he technically would still be an amateur until his first game as a pro. The hitch there might be an adverse ruling by officials of the International Olympics Committee who might not recognize his technical amateur status. 3. He could turn pro. Money would be the big factor in that decision.

There was a lot of pressure on Johnson from people on both sides of the issue. Those who were against it included most of the people in Michigan—at least those who were basketball fans. One businessman from Grand Rapids paid $1,200 for a full-page ad in *The Michigan State News* that said in part, "We've ... learned in the marketplace of life that a college degree ... will be with you always." Anyone in East Lansing with even a touch of town spirit wanted him to stay at MSU. And, of course, everyone at MSU wanted him there at least another year. His coach, Jud Heathcote, and MSU's athletic director, Joe Kearney, also thought it would be in his best interests to stay but, of course, it would be in their best interests, too. His teammates wanted him to stay. Jay Vincent thought he should play college ball two more years because it was fun. "What's better than that?" Vincent asked simply.

Earvin's father and Charles Tucker were no longer so concerned with his staying in college. His father, who had been most strongly opposed to his going pro the year before, now felt he was ready to play pro ball. Naturally, Mr. Johnson was well aware of what the money from a pro contract would mean, but he was not about to let Earvin "sell himself cheap." If an NBA team offered $500,000 a year for four years, Earvin should turn pro. Otherwise, he should stay in college.

Earvin himself had pretty much decided to turn pro. His main concern was how his mother would feel about his leaving college. They had a talk about it, and he promised that he would go to summer school and complete the necessary credits just as soon as his schedule would allow.

The NBA draft was to be held in late June, but Earvin Johnson was pretty sure which team he would be playing with long before that time. Several seasons before, the Los Angeles Lakers had obtained the right to a first-round pick in the 1979 draft from the Utah Jazz (which at that time was the New Orleans Jazz). If the Lakers won the coin toss that decided which team would pick first, they would be able to pick whomever they wanted.

There was no question that the Lakers wanted Magic. Representatives from the Lakers met with the Johnsons, Charles Tucker, and Earvin's agent, Charles Andrews of Chicago, to negotiate the terms of the signing. They finally agreed on a deal that called for $600,000 a year for four years. Earvin knew that Larry Bird had signed with the Boston Celtics for $650,000 a year, but he was pretty happy with the agreement anyway. As he told Douglas Looney of *Sports Illustrated,* "Now, I don't think I'm worth as much as Bird. Let's be honest. He played longer, has gotten the experience and the accolades and besides, wow, he's a white superstar. Basketball sure needs him."

Contract negotiations are kept secret, so no one but the parties involved knows just how the $600,000 figure was arrived at. Perhaps the Lakers representatives argued that Larry Bird, three years older than Johnson and having finished college, was a more mature player. And, after all, he had been named Player of the Year for the 1978-1979 college season. It may also have had something to do with the fact that Earvin was going "hardship" in order to turn pro.

"Hardship" was a designation given in cases where a player turned pro before finishing college. Formerly, NBA rules had not allowed teams to draft undergraduates because it was felt that players benefited from the four years of experience playing college ball (also the colleges didn't want the pro teams to take away their best players). When the American Basketball Association had started back in 1967, it had adopted a hardship rule whereby players in college, or even players right out of high school, could be drafted if they could show that it was a financial hardship for their families to keep them in college, or send them to college in the first place. All of a sudden, half the college players in the nation were having a hard time paying for college!

The NBA refused to adopt a similar rule, even in self-defense (The ABA got a lot of potential NBA players through the hardship draft). But in 1976, when the ABA merged into the NBA, a hardship rule was part of the agreement under which the two leagues would join forces. To this day, it is used, but only sparingly. In general, it takes two or three years for players to adjust to the pro game after they have quit college before graduating. Even if they develop into sound pro players, some of them never develop a stable emotional attitude toward their job. They never develop the proper sense of responsibility. There was probably some feeling within the Lakers organization that two more years of college play would not have hurt Johnson's game and that for a couple of years at least he wasn't worth quite as much as a player with four years of college play under his belt.

Six hundred thousand dollars a year was nothing to sneeze at. It was more than the Johnson family, with eight children, had ever expected to see. The first thing Earvin wanted to do was to buy his family a new house and do something nice for each of his brothers and sisters. Dr. Tucker and his parents advised him not to spend the money before he even had it. They reminded him that making so much money was serious business. There were taxes to think about, and if he did not invest his money wisely the government would take about half of it. The money should be invested so that Earvin would have it in the future. At the age of 19, healthy and strong, Earvin felt as if he could play basketball forever, but there was always the possibility of injury. Even if he was not injured, his body would become less lithe and supple, his bones and muscles would become less strong. By the time he was in his early thirties he would have to start thinking about retiring from the game. He would have a chance then to go on to a new career, but if he was smart and had invested his basketball salary carefully he would have something to show for his playing years besides trophies and yellowed newspaper clippings.

When the NBA draft opened on June 25th, there wasn't much suspense as far as the signing of Magic Johnson was concerned. Earlier, Los Angeles had won the coin flip with Chicago for the first pick in the draft. In the Grand Ballroom of the Plaza Hotel in New York City, the name "Earvin Johnson" was spoken loudly and clearly by the Lakers' representative. Moments later, Greg Kelser was drafted by the Detroit Pistons. As other names were spoken and other picks were made, the full reality of the moment began to dawn on Earvin. "Wow," he said to himself, "on the same team as *Kareem Abdul-Jabbar!*"

PART 3

Professional

Chapter 8

Professional basketball is a lot different from the school or playground game. First of all, it is a job. Even if you love playing basketball more than anything else in the world, it is still hard to play night after night during the long NBA season. Magic was used to a school basketball schedule of 20 to 30 games in five months. In the coming season with the Lakers, he would be playing at least 82 games in six months.

Many of those games would be in other cities. There would be long road trips, and that was something else Magic had not experienced before. A couple of away games a month in college basketball just does not prepare a player for the hardships of the NBA road schedule. Imagine being on the road for 12 to 13 straight days, traveling by plane and bus, having to think about scheduling delays, waiting around in airports, worrying that you won't have enough time to practice or to get a good night's sleep before you have to play the next game. And, imagine sleeping in strange hotel beds that are built for six-foot tall people; eating hotel food for a week straight; trying to figure out what channel your favorite television show is on in a strange city, and—most difficult of all—adjusting to the "jet lag" you feel when you leave Los Angeles at 10 o'clock in the morning, fly five hours to get to New York City, find out it's noon when you arrive and that you've lost three hours along the way.

There is more to the hardships of the road than such discomforts. It is also hard playing on a strange court, and it is even harder playing in front of a crowd that is rooting against you. There would be times when even if you made a great assist or shot a beautiful basket only a few people would applaud. It would be tough, too, being at the free-throw line and hearing a chorus of boos as the fans of the home team try to make you miss that extra-point shot. It is no accident that even the best teams lose a high percentage of their road games.

The long road trips became so exhausting that at the end of the 1978-79 season NBA officials decided to change the schedule so that there would be fewer of them. Before the schedule was changed each team played each other team four times, two times on each home court. This sometimes meant playing a game in Los Angeles one night, in Philadelphia the next, and in New York the next. Not even the best team in the league could play well on that kind of schedule. When the schedule was changed for the 1979-1980 season, it was decided that the teams in a conference would play each other more often, and that there would be fewer games with teams in other conferences. The Lakers would be playing the Seattle Supersonics six times in the regular season, three times on each court. They would be playing the New York Knicks only twice, once on each court. This new schedule would cut down on the long road trips. It was hoped that these changes would generate more fan enthusiasm, since it was felt that fans were more interested in rivalries between teams from the same area of the country than in contests with teams from far away.

As a result, Magic Johnson was going to have an easier first year in the NBA than rookies of the past few years had experienced. This did not mean it would not be a difficult adjustment for him just the same. But Magic was not the kind of person to let these problems worry him all that much. He loved basketball, and he was going to get paid for playing it—what greater luck could he have? He knew the NBA season was a long one, but he was pretty sure he could maintain his energy and enthusiasm for most of it. "It's impossible to play hard for 82 games," he realized. "But I bet I can play hard in at least 70."

Actually Earvin faced a lot of changes and adjustments even before the basketball season began because he was going to be far away from home for an extended period of time for the first time in his life. He was glad that he would be making enough money so he could call home pretty much anytime he felt like it. The family would be staying in East Lansing. Mrs. Johnson recalls that "Some people thought that when he went out West, we'd be going, too." But there was never any serious discussion of that idea because Earvin's four younger sisters were still in school, and his parents both had their jobs. Mrs. Johnson had been working in the Lansing schools for ten years, and Mr. Johnson had been with Oldsmobile for 24 years. Things would be different without Earvin in the Johnson home—a lot quieter, for one thing. "Actually," Mrs. Johnson said at the time, "things are calm now compared to when he was in high school and led his team to the state title. Of course, that last year at Michigan State was tough on us all with reporters calling all the time."

Earvin's other concern was how he would get along with his new teammates and how he would fit in the Lakers organization. He knew the team would be going through many changes. Six other new players would be starting with the team, and it would be very important for all of them to be able to work together. He also knew that the veteran Lakers had a reputation for being cool and playing cool. Of course, that was the exact opposite of the way he behaved and played. He didn't want his new teammates to think he was some sort of silly kid. He hoped they would appreciate his enthusiasm.

Earvin's concern was not unfounded. The Los Angeles Lakers team he was joining was not exactly known for enthusiasm, or for inspiring much emotion in its fans. Bruce Newman of *Sports Illustrated* summed it up, "If the entire emotional content of one of the Lakers' recent seasons were on film, it could be screened during one cycle of the 24-second clock."

It was a fact that the Lakers had not had many speedy, ball-handling guards in the past few seasons. The fast-break was not their style. Instead, the tone of their game reflected the style of play of the three major players—Kareem Abdul-Jabbar, Jamaal Wilkes, and Adrian Dantley—who were slow and deliberate as they focused on getting the ball to Abdul-Jabbar, at the high post, where he could either pass off to an open man or go in either for a loping lay-up or to lob the ball into the basket with one of his well known "sky hook" shots.

Jabbar himself had not felt very enthusiastic on the court for a long time. He was 31 years old and had been in the NBA for ten seasons by the time Magic joined the Lakers. Jabbar had won every individual prize available to a professional player, and he had been on championship teams several times. By now basketball had become more of a job than a game to him. Quiet, even aloof from his teammates, he did what he was paid to do and that was all. He did not seem to have any "emotional

---

Laker Magic Johnson signals to a teammate. *Los Angeles Lakers*

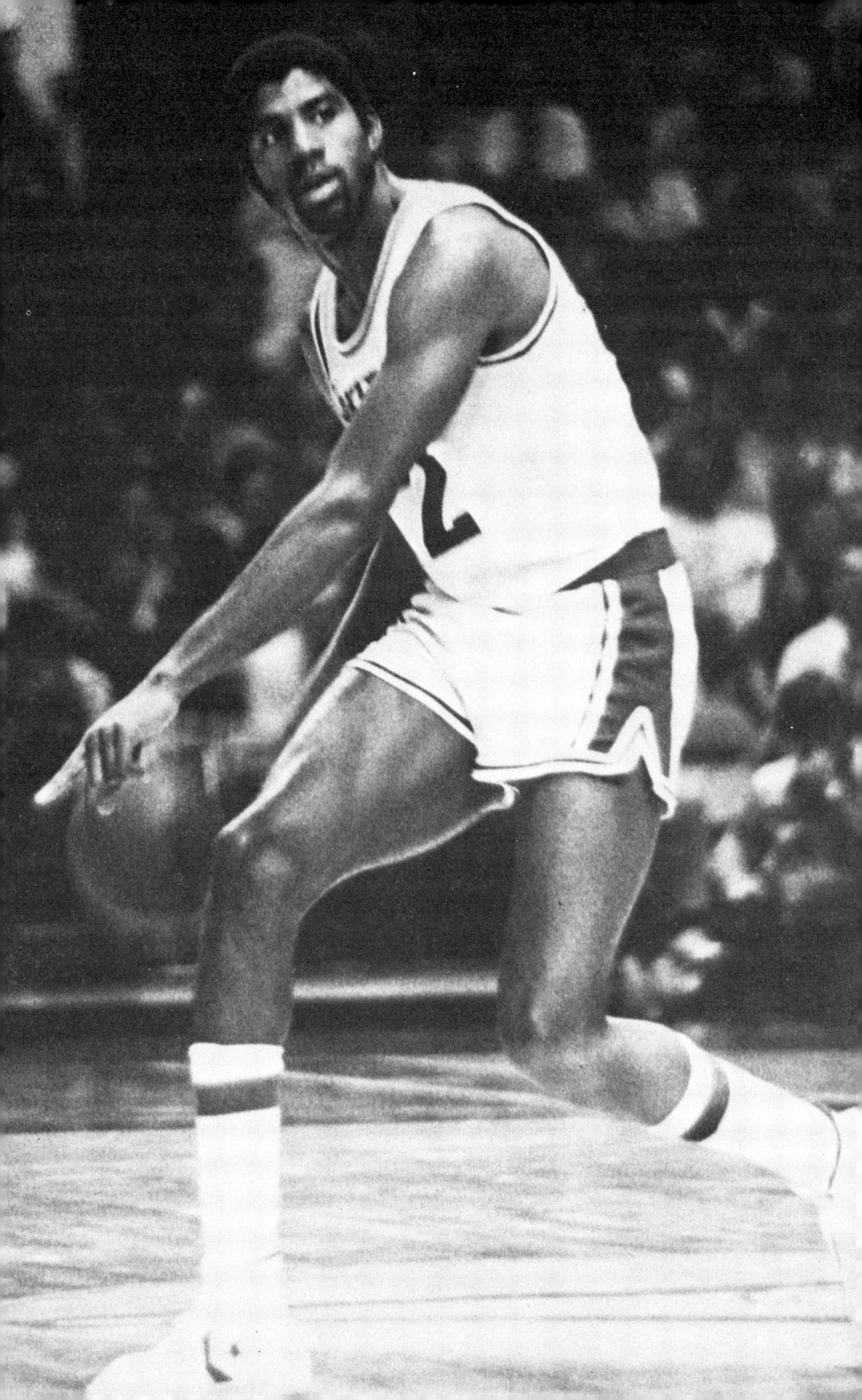

investment" in how the Lakers did. In fact, he seemed rather bored with it all.

More than anything else, Earvin Johnson was concerned about playing with Kareem Abdul-Jabbar and about how he would get along with the big man. He'd heard that Abdul-Jabbar was unemotional and that he didn't work hard. To someone as enthusiastic and energetic as Earvin, a person like that was difficult to understand.

The summer of 1979 was full of new experiences for Earvin. Just finding a place to live was an adventure. He was astounded at the high cost of renting an apartment in Los Angeles. Back in East Lansing he and Andy Wells had shared the $255-a-month rent for a large and comfortable place. In Los Angeles, that kind of rent would just about pay for a closet. On the advice of Dr. Tucker and others, Earvin decided to buy a condominium apartment. It would be an investment, and he wouldn't just be throwing away rent money. Earvin, who wasn't too happy about leaving all his friends back in Michigan, wanted a place that was big enough to accommodate them all, so they could "come in and take over." Dr. Tucker and Lakers' owner Jerry Buss looked for a place just big enough for his parents to stay comfortably when they came to visit. Tucker was not worried that Earvin would turn to drugs or alcohol when he was on his own. But he was worried that his young friend would party too much and be a sucker for hangers-on who pretended to be his good friends but who really just wanted to take advantage of his good fortune. There are lots of sports "groupies," and Tucker knew enough about them to stand firm on the question of apartment size. "They eat at you," he told Earvin.

Once Earvin had bought a smaller apartment than he had

envisioned, there was still furniture to buy and a new neighborhood and city to discover. Los Angeles was much more spread out than Lansing. Simply learning to drive on all those freeways was a new experience.

Earvin also had to get used to being a "star." Hundreds of companies offered him money to endorse their products and to appear in their advertisements. He was amazed at all the attention. "I've become the most businessed 19-year-old in the country," he exclaimed at the end of July. By that time he was beginning to feel the lack of privacy that comes with stardom. His time just didn't seem to be his own anymore.

His "real life" schedule during those first few months was hectic. He played in a rookie league game in Los Angeles. (NBA rookies play each other a lot before their first pro season to get into NBA shape and learn the pro game.) Next he went to San Antonio for another rookie game and from there, he went to Boston for an athletic shoe convention, and then on to New York to take part in a playground basketball clinic. He went home to Michigan for a few days after that before returning to Los Angeles to do some more practicing with his new team. Another rookie game followed in Houston, after which he went home to Michigan again. From there he went to Mississippi to visit relatives on his father's side of the family, returned home, packed up the last of his things, and moved to Los Angeles. By now it was late August, but there was no time to rest. The Los Angeles Lakers' preseason training was about to begin in earnest, and Earvin Johnson's most important adjustment—to all his new teammates—was still ahead of him.

Earvin was not the only new member of the Lakers organization. In fact, there had been a lot of changes made. There was the new owner, Jerry Buss, who wanted some excitement from his new team and was prepared to pay for it. There were new players. Spencer Haywood from the Utah Stars replaced Adrian Dantley, Jim Chones came from the Cleveland Cavaliers, and there were four other players who would be wearing Lakers uniforms for the first time.

The team also had a new coach, Jack McKinney, who had been assistant coach of the Portland Trailblazers, and before that an assistant coach with the Milwaukee Bucks when Kareem Abdul-Jabbar was with the team. Since this was McKinney's first job as head coach, he was a rookie in a way, too. But he had a big advantage over a rookie player. He was the coach, and it would be up to the others to adjust to him.

Earvin Johnson had kept his hand in the game that summer, playing even when he wasn't scheduled for rookie games or exhibition games because he knew how easy it was to get out of shape. He also wanted to be comfortable with the NBA game, which was different in several respects from NCAA basketball. The 48-minute-long college game was divided into four 12-minute quarters while an NBA game was 60 minutes long and divided into four 15-minute quarters. The zone defense, which was legal in NCAA play, was illegal in the NBA. In the NBA you couldn't just establish position in one area of the floor and stay there, which meant a lot more moving around on defense. There would also be more moving around on offense. In college basketball, the team with the ball can take as long as it wants to get off a shot. This is not so in the NBA, which has a 24-second shooting clock. The clock is set when a team gets possession of the ball. If the team does not get a shot off in 24 seconds, a buzzer sounds and the team automatically loses possession.

"Rookie" Magic Johnson greets "Skyhook" Kareem Abdul-Jabbar.

Wide World Photos

The NBA game is much rougher than the college game, as anyone will find out if they get under the basket with some of those big NBA players. It is no wonder that the biggest and strongest players are called "enforcers." The NBA game can get downright dirty under the basket, with lots of elbowing and shoving.

One rule that would be new to all NBA players, except those who had come over to the league from the defunct American Basketball Association, was the three-point basket. During its brief existence it was a rule in the ABA that if you made a basket from 22 feet away or more, you would score three points instead of the usual two. The NBA had resisted that rule for years, but by 1979 the league was losing attendance, and the three-point basket rule was adopted in the hope that it would make the game more exciting and attract more fans.

There was a lot of talk around the league that year about attracting more fans to NBA games. It was hoped that some of the exciting rookies like Magic Johnson would increase game attendance. It had been shown that such talk was not idle back in the summer. In his very first appearance in a Laker rookie game at California State University in Los Angeles, 3,000 people had come to see him—and several hundred more had tried unsuccessfully to get in.

Usually, fewer than 1,000 people went to those summer rookie games. And, the people at this game were not just autograph-seeking youngsters. Four head coaches were there, including the new Lakers head coach, Jack McKinney.

Earvin had only practiced twice before the game. Although he was not in the starting lineup he scored 24 points and made nine assists in the 28 minutes that he played. He was not totally satisfied with his play, but the spectators had no reason to doubt that he deserved his nickname. Both Lakers' owner Jerry

Buss and Coach McKinney were smiling broadly, thinking that if Magic could perform like that after only two practices, it would be really exciting to see what he could do when the season started.

Once the preseason training camp began, Earvin deliberately held himself in check. He realized that he would be watched closely by his new teammates. There had been an awful lot of publicity about him, and he knew the veteran players would be skeptical of a kid who had just turned 20 but whom the press was hailing as the savior of the team, if not of the entire NBA. So he decided to keep a low profile, to watch his new teammates closely, and to get to know how they played. He was pleasantly surprised to find that the others were treating him the same way, and he was especially pleased to see that Abdul-Jabbar was not nearly as aloof as he was said to be. The Lakers center worked very hard. And he didn't just go through the motions. He cracked jokes and got mad just like the other players. Jabbar also seemed genuinely interested in the rookie Johnson.

The sportswriters who attended the preseason practice sessions were not very impressed with Earvin's play. "Less than spectacular" was the way one writer put it. But Earvin was only doing what the whole team had to do, which was to learn to play with one another. In fact, Coach McKinney wasn't expecting his team to really start to "click" until about midseason. The players on a team have to get used to one another; they have to learn each man's playing style and adjust their own styles to the others. Earvin Johnson was a passer. He had become famous in college for making "no look" passes and finding his intended receiver. In order to make such passes successfully, he had to know how his teammates moved. For their part, his teammates had to learn to play with him, and

Magic starts his glide for a lay-up against the Golden State Warriors.
Wide World Photos

especially to be aware that he might shoot the ball their way at any moment.

At first, Earvin just could not seem to make his passes connect. He'd find an open man, throw the ball, and see it bounce into empty space. Sometimes, he'd make a quick, no-look pass, and see it chunk a teammate in the forehead. But he didn't give up. He kept on trying, and gradually his passes started to connect. Coach McKinney saw enough progress to decide that Earvin, even though he was six-foot-eight and tall enough to be a forward, should be the chief ball-handling guard, the point guard who leads the fast break and sets up the offense. It was guard Norm Nixon who had to develop his technique of moving without the ball. This decision didn't please Nixon, who was used to being the ball-handler, but there wasn't much point in arguing with the coach.

The more he practiced with his new team, the more Earvin Johnson loosened up. He cracked jokes, he made spectacular dives to save the ball from going out of bounds, and he smiled that wonderful smile of his. His teammates couldn't help but smile back, even after they were bopped on the head by one of his passes. There was a sense of fun on the court, and a sense of camaraderie that had not been felt among the Lakers for a long time. Their play as a team was still somewhat ragged, but they could see improvement and they were willing to keep trying. Everyone was looking forward to the start of the regular season.

Chapter 9

Rookie Magic Johnson's regular season with the Lakers began on October 12, 1979, in San Diego, California, against the San Diego Clippers. Earvin couldn't seem to get started at first. He was still not used to the extreme physicality of the pro game, and he was held to one point in his first 17 minutes of play. "I was in a daze," he said afterward. "I was in another world. The coach took me out and it was a good thing he did." Sitting on the bench, Earvin couldn't help remembering how he had "tightened up" during his first college basketball game. Was the same thing happening now? It just wouldn't do to be so tense. Here he was doing what he had dreamed about for years, and he decided that he was going to enjoy it.

A different rookie Johnson returned to the game. He knew exactly where he was and what he had to do. By the closing seconds of the game he had 26 points. Still, as the clock ticked down, he faced losing his first NBA game. There were only two seconds remaining and the Clippers not only led 102-101, but they had possession of the ball.

Suddenly a Clipper lost control and the ball went out of bounds. This gave the Lakers one more chance. The inbounds pass went straight to Jabbar, and with one of his famous sky-hook shots from the free-throw line, the Lakers center sank the ball home. Final score: Los Angeles 103, San Diego 102. Earvin was the second highest scorer for the Lakers. The team's owner was very pleased with his new rookie, saying, "I expect to do a lot of business with the magic Johnson makes."

Less than a week later, Earvin had to be carried off the court on a stretcher. The team was in Seattle playing the Supersonics. With a minute and a half left in the third quarter, both Earvin and Seattle's Dennis Johnson went up for a rebound, got tangled up, and fell to the court. Earvin grimaced in pain as he clutched his right knee. While time out was called for injury, a Sonics' team physician taped up the knee, and Earvin was carried off the court. Back in Los Angeles, Lakers' physicians diagnosed the injury as a sprain that would take about a week to heal. Eight days and three missed games later, Earvin was back in uniform against the Kansas City Kings. Although Coach McKinney decided to be careful with his rookie and only let him play 28 minutes, Earvin scored 26 points and led his team to a 116-104 win.

In the weeks that followed, Earvin lived up to all his preseason publicity again and again. He didn't always score a lot, and he made plenty of mistakes, but when he "clicked" he was spectacular. The Golden State Warriors beat the Lakers in a game on the Golden State home court November 7th, but the Warriors coach Al Attles was not very happy with the way his players had reacted to Johnson's passes. He described them as being "mesmerized"—practically stopping play in order to watch him. Johnson's own teammates sometimes found themselves reacting the same way. During the third quarter of a game against San Diego, with a five-point Laker lead, Magic got the ball at midcourt and fired a pass right between two Clippers to forward Jim Chones. Earvin had not seemed to notice Chones, and Chones was so deep in traffic that he was hardly looking for the pass. When the ball suddenly appeared in his hands, he was so startled that for an instant he just stared at it. Recovering quickly, he put it into the basket. As he made his way back down the floor on defense, Chones shook his head in disbelief. Earvin seemed to know where the ball was and was going to be, and where his teammates were going to be as well. He was able to give them the ball in the rhythm of their move so they could go right to the basket with it.

Magic was amazing. He had exceptional confidence for a rookie, and it wasn't the kind of youthful cockiness that gives a coach headaches, especially if the coach has enough faith in his rookie to let him take over when the time seems right. There was a game against the Phoenix Suns earlier in the season where, with the score tied and less than 30 seconds left to play, the Lakers got possession. McKinney ordered a time-out and started telling his team to run a play that would get the ball to forward Jamaal Wilkes. Earvin objected, saying that was a play the Suns would be expecting and ready to defend against. Why not pretend to look for Wilkes but get the ball to him, Earvin, for the final shot instead? It was a gamble, but Coach McKinney decided to try it. The ball was put in play, passed around, and with about a second remaining on the shot clock, Earvin took aim for the basket. Fouled in the act of shooting by a Phoenix player, he went to the free-throw line and made both shots. Los Angeles won the game by two points. Coach McKinney then remembered reading about how Magic often acted like a sort of assistant coach in college.

A week later Coach McKinney was injured off the court. In what was described as a freak accident, he fell off a bicycle he was riding near his home and suffered an injury to his head.

That meant his assistant coach Paul Westhead would take over. A former English literature teacher, the assistant coach was well liked by the players, but it would still be hard to adjust to a new coach. Although he tried to follow Coach McKinney's style as closely as possible, Westhead had his own style and his own way of doing things. Luckily, his style was one his players could appreciate.

Magic Johnson's reaction to the coaching change was to try even harder. He always wanted to win, but now he wanted to win both for Coach McKinney, lying in a hospital bed, and for Coach Westhead, who suddenly found the entire responsibility for the team on his shoulders. McKinney's accident occurred on Thursday, November 8th. The next day the Denver Nuggets came to town.

During the first half, the entire Lakers team seemed to be showing the effects of what had happened to their coach. They couldn't seem to do anything right. The Lakers and Coach Westhead seemed to be unsure of themselves. In fact, before the game started, Westhead told Kareem that if he got kicked out, Kareem was the coach. Westhead was afraid he might get too emotional and say something to an official that would get him ejected from the game. Westhead did not get ejected in the first half, but he did get emotional. The team was doing poorly, and by halftime Denver had a comfortable lead.

If there was ever a time for a locker-room pep talk, this was it. The team agreed that they were not playing the way they should be. They couldn't let Coach McKinney down, and they couldn't let Coach Westhead think he couldn't coach them. They came out roaring for the second half. Johnson and Nixon got the fast-break going, and by the end of regulation time the score was tied.

In the overtime period, Earvin just kept gathering steam. He

Darryl Dawkins of the Philadelphia 76ers and Magic Johnson of the Los Angeles Lakers go up for the rebound.   *United Press International Photos*

made eight straight baskets, leading his team to a 126-122 overtime victory. When the statistics were tallied, he learned that he had been credited not only with eight assists and six rebounds, but with 31 points, more points that he had ever scored in the NBA before. Beaming, he told Bruce Newman of *Sports Illustrated,* "When we started running, my confidence started to rise. That's when I knew it was time to deal on some people. When we're rolling and the break is going, I guess it looks as if I *am* performing magic out there. There are some nights I think I can do anything."

One thing Earvin rarely forgot was that he was part of a team. Most nights he was only as good as his teammates would allow him to be. There were times when individuals excelled— like the night Earvin scored 31 points. Most of the time, however, the Lakers played a remarkably well-balanced game. In the November 18th game against the Pacers in Indianapolis, for example, forward Jamaal Wilkes led the scoring with 21 points. Reserve guard Michael Cooper was right behind him with 20. Abdul-Jabbar, Johnson, and Spencer Haywood each had 14, Norm Nixon and Jim Chones had 12 each, and Marty Barnes had 11. Just as important were the assist statistics. The Lakers had 36 assists, compared to 21 for Indiana. The Lakers *team* won the game, which is what happened most of the time when they won. In years past, it had so often been up to Abdul-Jabbar to win. Now, the pressure was off him. He began to enjoy the game again.

Still, when it came to that unmeasurable quality—enjoyment— Earvin Johnson *was* the star. His enthusiasm was as contagious as his smile. He played all-out in nearly every game and, as the weeks passed, the rest of the team started to do the same. Now, when a loose ball bounced toward the boundary line, any Laker within 20 feet went after the save. Now, when a Laker made a great basket, or a fine pass, or a tough rebound, other Lakers showed their appreciation with a slap on the rear end, or a clenched-fist victory sign. All this was Magic's doing. He reacted to every good play as if it was a championship-clincher. He was his teammates' most enthusiastic cheerleader, and by midpoint in his rookie season he was in many ways the focus of the team.

His former college teammate, Greg Kelser, had not been so lucky. The Detroit Pistons' first draft choice had been plagued by injuries all season. When the Pistons went to Los Angeles to play the Lakers on December 14th, Kelser stayed behind. He did not play against his former partner in the lob and dunk when the Lakers went to the Detroit Silverdome on January 11th either. Suffering from ligament damage in his right ankle, Kelser was on the injured reserve list and had to miss five games. It was his second time on the list, and he had not played much at all since the season began. In fact, he had missed 21 of the Pistons' 43 games, and in the 22 games he had played, he had started in only five, averaged only 15 minutes of playing time, and had 7.9 points and 4.1 rebounds. On top of all that, the Pistons had the worst record in the NBA. "I guess I have to look at it from the standpoint that I've got age on my side," said Greg to a reporter for the *Detroit News*. "There are going to be a lot of chances to play Los Angeles." But he had been looking forward to playing on the same court with Earvin again, even if they were on opposite teams.

Earvin had been looking forward to playing on the same court with Greg, too. The former teammates had kept in touch. Earvin had felt badly about his great success when he talked with his friend and heard about his injury problems. Greg's problems reminded Earvin that injuries could really wreck an athlete's season, if not his entire career. At such times, it was hard to play all-out, risking injury every time he was on a court. But he put his worry in the back of his mind, knowing that the game of basketball is not a game that can be played cautiously.

By the end of December, Earvin Johnson was a rookie only because he was still in his first year. In just about every other way he was a veteran, and that included his behavior off the court as well as on. The fears of his family and advisers had proved unfounded. Magic was so busy playing and practicing that he didn't have time to party. When he did have some time to himself, he preferred quiet dates or listening to records by himself. He had made friends with some of his teammates, but he hadn't allowed groupies and hangers-on to complicate his life. He had adjusted so well to being away from the family and living on his own that he was in a position to give advice to his sister Evelyn, on adjusting.

Evelyn was a freshman at the University of South Carolina. She could have gone to Michigan State and stayed close to home, but she had decided her older brother was a tough act to follow. She had already experienced being in his shadow when she, too, was an All-Stater in basketball at Everett High. Everytime she broke a school record—even one of Earvin's—it just seemed to remind everyone of the great days when he was there. She wanted to make her own name and not just be known as "Magic Johnson's sister" or "Lady Magic." She had no trouble making the South Carolina women's basketball team, and did quite well, but by midseason she had become very homesick. One night she called her brother in Los Angeles and told him she was ready to quit.

Earvin advised Evelyn to stay. Don't be a quitter, he said. You're doing well out there. You shouldn't turn your back on your team. He told her she would call him, collect, any time she felt homesick or depressed, and she took him up on the offer. More often than not, she asked him for advice about basketball. She led her team to a third-place finish in the women's college basketball tournament with 21 points and decided to stop fighting her association with her brother. "I can't get rid of it," she said. "I just have to face up to it. I'm Magic's sister. They won't call me 'Sweet E,' just "Magic Something.'"

By early February 1980, the Lakers had a won-lost record of 39 and 17 and were just one game behind the Seattle Supersonics in the Pacific Division. In the entire NBA only the Boston Celtics and Philadelphia 76ers had better records than theirs. If the Lakers had been in their second season playing together as a team, they would probably have been in first place in the whole league.

They were still making adjustments. In a game that requires as much teamwork as pro basketball does, a group of players just can't "click" even after playing together for 55 games. And there is always the matter of ego. Most pro basketball players have healthy egos and feel that winning is up to them, which can destroy teamwork as easily as jealousy over publicity and playing time can.

Of all the Lakers, it was hardest for guard Norm Nixon to adjust to his new role on the team. But since the Lakers were winning twice as many games as they were losing, Nixon had been afraid to complain. It would have sounded as if he was just jealous. But there came a time in February when it became clear that other players, too, felt that Earvin Johnson was forgetting he had teammates to help him.

When the Lakers were behind, or when the score was too close for comfort, the rookie tended to play as if he was the only player on the team. In fast breaks, other Lakers would race down the floor to get good positions, then just stand there as Earvin took the ball all the way to the line. It wasn't selfishness that made him do this; it was his concentration on winning? but it still wasn't good for the team. In an away game against the New Jersey Nets in early February, the assistant coach, Pat Riley, pulled Earvin aside and told him he had to watch for his teammates and pass off to them when he saw they were open.

Earvin got upset. "I can't do nothin' right," he said, throwing up his arms in despair. But he didn't just brood about being corrected. He thought about what the coach had said and decided there was probably something to it. From then on he looked for his teammates, and by April Norm Nixon was praising his rookie teammate for making the effort to give the ball to the others more often and saying that he and Johnson complemented each other in their play.

The major thing that the other players had to adjust to in Johnson was his enthusiasm, which caused him to make mistakes. Anyone who plays all-out as Magic does is bound to make mistakes. In the first part of the season, his teammates would groan when he threw a wild pass, but as they won more and more games—many of the thanks to Earvin—they realized his mistakes should not be cause for worry. If he threw the ball away, so what? Chances were he would make up for it the next time down the court. "He wins a lot of games just on his effort," said Jim Chones. "He goes out there and says, 'I want to win and I'm not gonna be bothered by all those superficial things.' "

By March, the Lakers had a won-lost record that made them playoff contenders. But most observers saw more in their future than just getting into the playoffs. After all, the Lakers had made the playoffs before. This year, they looked like championship contenders, a sure bet to give the 1979 champion

Laker Magic Johnson drives through the Cleveland Cavaliers.

Wide World Photos

Seattle Supersonics a run for the Pacific Division title.

In every way the Lakers were an exciting team. One of the reasons for the excitement was owner Jerry Buss. He was not just a businessman who looked at how the team was doing in terms of profit and loss. He was a real basketball fan. He made his presence felt behind the scenes, in the locker room. From his special box seat he whistled and cheered and booed like the most avid rooter. He was close to the players and made them feel he really cared about them, which did a great deal for their morale.

Of course, another reason for the excitement about the Lakers was Kareem Abdul-Jabbar. Although he had never had a poor season in the NBA, the 1979-1980 season was turning out to be one of his very best. He felt good, he was playing superbly, and he seemed to be enjoying the game more than he had in years.

One of the reasons for Kareem's enjoyment, and a third reason why the Lakers were doing so well, was Magic Johnson. Abdul-Jabbar quickly got over his reservations about Earvin. Magic told Abdul-Jabbar that they were going to have fun, and he made the games fun. Their relationship now extended off the court. Earvin looked to Kareem for advice and openly admired the older player. Theirs was very much like a big-brother, little-brother relationship.

Earvin's enthusiasm had not lessened at all in the course of his first, grueling NBA season. The coolness of most of the older Lakers had not rubbed off on him; instead, his excitement and determination to win had rubbed off on them. Once, after Abdul-Jabbar sank an 18-foot skyhook to win a game, Magic had actually leaped upon the startled center, causing the whole team to break up laughing. He always managed to have fun. If his team had a comfortable lead, he'd cut up a bit, throwing the ball behind his back, waving to the girls, or flashing his famous grin at the scorekeepers after he'd made a basket. "Magic has such an infectious, happy attitude that he's imparted it to the players," said Jerry Buss. "They're happy while they're playing, and they're very intent on winning."

Of course, Magic had brought more than just enthusiasm to the team. By mid-March he had a respectable scoring average of 18.4, and he led all other NBA guards with an average of seven rebounds per game. When the Lakers made the Western Conference playoffs there were very few observers who did not give a big share of the credit to him.

Chapter 10

In 1978, Seattle had knocked the Lakers out of the playoffs in the first round. The next year, they had beat them in the conference semifinals and then gone on to win the NBA championship. Naturally, the Lakers felt it was their turn now.

The series consisted of seven games. Seattle won the first, but Los Angeles roared back to win the second and third with exceptionally balanced play. Abdul-Jabbar was unstoppable, with 33 points one night and 36 the next. In fact, all the Lakers were playing well. Jamaal Wilkes came out of a brief shooting slump by the time of the second game, and both Norm Nixon and Earvin Johnson were scoring in double figures.

For much of the fourth game it looked as if Seattle was going to be able to catch up and tie the series. The Lakers were missing shots and although they improved as the game went on, they were trailing 75-72 as the last period began. Then Magic came alive, playing as if it was his last game ever. He pounded down the court on the fast break, passed off to his man, and dove for every loose ball. In a steal attempt, he injured his right upper arm and had to leave the game, but his teammates kept up the pace he'd set. Before leaving the game Johnson had piled up 15 points, 13 rebounds, and six assists. The Lakers won 98-93.

Now the Sonics had their backs to the wall. If they didn't win the next game, their basketball season would be over. By halftime in the fifth game they were ahead 62-54. Kareem Abdul-Jabbar did not like that situation at all. Not usually one to play coach and give his team pep talks, Kareem decided this was a time to step out of character. In the locker room at halftime, he gave his teammates a brief, but thorough scolding. They couldn't play the way they had in the first half and expect to win. They were overconfident because they had a 3-1 edge in the series. But overconfidence was going to cause them to lose. "It's been a long season," he said. "Let's not let it slip away now." As Earvin said later, "He's like E.F. Hutton. When he talks, everybody listens."

A different Lakers team went out on the court in the second half. Within six minutes they had tied the score at 70-all. Trailing 98-97 with three-and-a-half minutes left in the game, the Lakers scored 12 of the next 16 points. When the buzzer sounded, the score was 109-102, Magic was hugging Kareem, and Kareem, with a smile as big as Magic's, was holding up his right forefinger to signal that the Lakers were Number One.

"Those last two and a half minutes were a microcosm of our season," said Coach Westhead. "We were playing tenacious defense, Magic was hanging on the boards, Kareem was throwing in skyhooks, Jamaal hitting jumpers, and Norman wheeling and dealing." For the first time since 1973, the Los Angeles Lakers would be in the final round of the NBA championship playoffs.

Meanwhile, back in the East, the Boston Celtics had been defeated by the Philadelphia 76ers in the Eastern Division championship playoff series. The season was over for the other much-heralded NBA rookie, Larry Bird. Bird received what amounted to a consolation prize when he was named NBA Rookie of the year.

Johnson was not too thrilled that the award went to Bird. The two had been compared for so long that when one received an award, it was natural for everyone to say in the same breath that the other had not. Bird's rookie season with the Celtics had been outstanding. He had averaged 21.3 points and 10.4 rebounds, and he certainly deserved the award. Magic Johnson knew this, and was the first to say it. But somehow, he thought he'd played well enough to share the Rookie of the Year title. Still, if it was a choice between playing in the NBA championship series and winning Rookie of the Year, he had no doubt about what he would choose. He wouldn't change places with Larry Bird for anything.

The Philadelphia 76ers were in the same position as the Lakers in many ways. They had not won an NBA championship in years. Led by star forward Julius Erving, they were a talented team, and they were as determined as the Lakers not to miss another chance at the NBA crown. The seven-game championship series was sure to be an exciting one, and most odds-makers were saying that it would not be decided until the seventh game.

In the first contest, played in Los Angeles, the two teams practically traded baskets for the first half. When the halftime buzzer sounded the score was tied. But the Lakers followed their custom and came out strong in the second half, scoring the first 12 points of the third period and holding the 76ers to just three field goals in the entire 15 minutes. At the start of the last period, the score was 78-62. Led by Dr. J., the 76ers came to within four points, but they couldn't rally enough to win. Los Angeles won 109-102. Abdul-Jabbar had a game-high 33 points and 14 rebounds. Johnson had 16 points, 10 assists, and nine rebounds. After the game, Julius Erving said, "The Lakers gamble more than any other club I've seen. Today it paid off for them, but I'd like to see them continue to gamble." The 76ers won the second game that was played in Los Angeles, 107-104.

With the series tied at one-all, both teams packed up and flew to Philadelphia. For the 76ers it was a homecoming. For the Lakers, it was the prospect of two games on an unfriendly court—so unfriendly, in fact, that the Lakers hadn't won a game there since 1975. They had already lost once at home. They would have to win at least once in Philadelphia to stay alive in the series. To make it worse, they would be playing one man short because Spencer Haywood, their power forward, was suspended for disciplinary reasons after the second game.

The Lakers won the first game in Philadelphia, 111-101, on great offensive and defensive rebounding. Jabbar had 14 rebounds, Wilkes 12, and Johnson 11. But Philadelphia came back in the next game and, although Earvin scored a game-high 28 points, the 76ers displayed fine teamwork and pulled the game out 105-102.

The series was now tied at two games apiece. There had been two games in Los Angeles and two in Philadelphia. Since it was a series with an uneven number of games, in the interests of fairness it was now necessary for the two teams to shuttle back and forth from one coast to another, playing just one game in each city. Both teams were tired after an 82-game regular season plus all their division playoff games. Earvin Johnson was beginning to wonder what the world was like outside airports, airplanes, and basketball courts. But he boarded the plane to Los Angeles with his team happy, at least, to be going home to a friendly court.

The Lakers won their game at home, the fifth of the series, 108-103, but the win cost them their star center. In the third period, Kareem Abdul-Jabbar went up for a rebound, got tangled up with other players, and crashed to the floor injuring his left ankle. He sat out the remaining minutes of the period. The score was so close that Earvin naturally felt under pressure to step up his own playing. "I wanted the ball. I wanted to take over, "he said later. "We knew we couldn't get our heads down with Kareem injured. The team had to keep playing basketball and get more intense." The Lakers, led by Earvin, extended their lead from two points to eight.

Kareem returned to the game in the fourth quarter. The score was still close, and everyone knew the team needed him. With the series tied, this game in Los Angeles was a "must-win" for the Lakers. If they lost, they would have to go back to Philadelphia down one game, and nobody wanted to do that. Kareem went back in and helped his team win, scoring 14 of his 40 points on the bad ankle, including a three-point play with 33 seconds left to break a 103-103 tie.

Although he had just a sprained ankle, the big center's play was clearly affected. Some important decisions had to be made about his playing in the remaining games of the series. It was decided that since the Lakers were one game ahead, they could afford to play without Kareem in the sixth game in Philadelphia. He could rest his ankle for a couple of days, and if the Lakers lost, he would be able to play in the seventh and final game in Los Angeles. "It should be interesting," Coach Westhead said to John Papaneck of *Sports Illustrated*. "Pure democracy. The king's on leave. We'll go with the slim line."

Once that decision had been made, there were other important decisions to be made. Kareem's absence would leave a big gap in the forward line. Coach Westhead couldn't just bring a reserve forward off the bench to fill it. So, the Lakers coaches sat down and did some major rearranging. In the sixth game, Michael Cooper, the reserve forward and sixth man on the team, would start in the backcourt with Norm Nixon. On defense, six-foot-eleven forward Jim Chones would play center, and Magic Johnson would move from guard to forward. But on offense, Chones would return to his forward position, and Magic Johnson would play center. It was the kind of gamble that Julius Erving had mentioned as typical of the Lakers. A lot of people thought Westhead was crazy and blamed it on the fact that he had "read too many books."

The Lakers did not learn that Kareem was staying behind until they arrived at the airport for the flight to Philadelphia. They were surprised to find out that he wouldn't be with them; they were astonished to learn about the lineup and position changes planned for them.

Earvin was used to being switched around a bit. In a couple of games against Philadelphia he and Norm Nixon had exchanged roles so that Nixon, who was smaller and faster, could play Philadelphia's smaller and faster guards. But center? He had not played center since his days at Everett High. And he had never been called upon to fill the shoes of a player like Kareem Abdul-Jabbar.

It was a subdued Lakers team that boarded the plane to Philadelphia on the afternoon of May 15th. Their big guy wasn't with them. They were not afraid of losing without him, or at least they told themselves they were not. But it would be hard to make up for the loss of his per game average of 33.4 points, 13.6 rebounds, and 4.6 blocked shots. Besides, with Haywood still under suspension, the Lakers were missing two key players and had only seven regulars in uniform. And it wouldn't seem right not to have Jabbar with them after all that the team had been through together. As Earvin put it, "The

Magic goes up against Dennis Artray of the Chicago Bulls.

Wide World Photos

thought of winning it without him isn't sad, but it's something close to it."

There was really little question in Earvin's mind that the team would win in Philadelphia. In his view, they had to do it for Kareem, and he was taking his special responsibility for that effort very seriously. He asked to wear Abdul-Jabbar's number, 33. In this situation, when he was playing in Kareem's position, he just felt he ought to wear the big man's number, which he was allowed to do. The same went for Kareem's seat on the plane. Kareem always takes the first seat in the first row on the left-hand side of the plane, so when the team boarded the plane for Philadelphia, there was Magic sitting in the first seat. If he was going to be Kareem-for-a-day, he was going to do it right.

By the time the Lakers were about to go out on the floor of the Philadelphia Spectrum, the whole team was beginning to feel like Earvin did. Coach Westhead realized that wasn't good. "Everyone expects an emotional game because we haven't got Kareem," he told his players. "But we didn't come here for courage. We came here to win."

The Lakers surprised the 76ers at the opening tip-off. Instead of Jim Chones as jumping center, there was the rookie Magic Johnson. And not only was he there, but he was giggling! He just couldn't believe he was at center. "I didn't know whether to stand with my right foot forward or my left," he later told John Papaneck of *Sports Illustrated*. "Didn't know when I should jump or where I should tap it if I got it . . . I looked at Caldwell Jones, the 76ers' center and realized he's 7'1" and he's got arms that make him around 9'5". So I just decided to jump up and down quick, then work on the rest of my game."

As expected, Caldwell Jones won the tip. But the Lakers scored the first seven points before the 76ers finally got started. The score was close until about halfway through the second quarter, when Julius Earving and Steve Mix led a spurt that put Philadelphia ahead 52-44. Westhead called time-out, told his team to run more and get more rebounds, and by halftime the score was 60-all.

In the Lakers's locker room, the unspoken agreement was that they were doing very well without Kareem, but they could do even better. In fact, why not go for it? Magic, who had been as enthusiastic as ever during that first half, decided to cheerlead as never before.

The Lakers were out for blood as they returned for the start of the second half. Magic had the first field goal, and the team went on to score the first 14 points of the period, cheered on by their teammate, Magic. He handed out high-five handshakes, hugged any Laker within reach, jumped wildly, and raised a clenched fist to the Spectrum ceiling every time they made a good play. By the end of the period, the Lakers had scored 33 points for a ten-point lead 93-83. The 76ers rallied in the fourth period and three times got to within one basket of a tie. With five minutes and 12 seconds remaining, the Lakers launched a blistering shooting barrage, scoring 20 points to the 76ers' six.

With 2:22 left to go and the contest pretty well sewed up, Magic called his first time-out of the season. "I was exhausted," he said later. "We ran so much." But he scored nine points in those last 2:22 minutes. When the buzzer sounded, the scoreboard showed 123-107. The Los Angeles Lakers were the champions of the NBA.

Amid the shouting and back-slapping in the Lakers' locker room, it was suddenly discovered that they lacked the traditional ingredient for a victory celebration. Whoever was in charge of things had evidently not had much faith in the team's ability to win without Jabbar: there wasn't a drop of champagne!

If ever a team deserved champagne, it was that Lakers team. Jamaal Wilkes had scored 37 points, Jim Chones had been outstanding on defense. Every one of the players had contributed, and the game will long be remembered as a classic of talent and teamwork. But Magic Johnson was the man of the hour. He had done a stupendous job, played his best NBA game ever: 47 minutes, 14-for-23 from the field, 14-for-14 at the foul line, 15 rebounds, seven assists, three steals, and 42 points. He had played center, forward, guard. "I was trying to name a new position," he said later, "but I couldn't come up with a new name. I guess you can just call me the new 'CFG (for center-forward-guard) Rover.' I was really just roaming around." The people who were to pick the Most Valuable Player for the series had thought all along that it would be Abdul-Jabbar, if the Lakers won, or Julius Earving, if the 76ers did. But after Johnson's performance in that sixth game, there was no question that he was M.V.P.

Coach Westhead kept calling him Houdini and Mr. Opportunity. Philadelphia Coach Billy Cunningham said, "If you ask me to compare him with Larry Bird, I'd have to take Johnson." Magic, besieged by well-wishers and reporters, was as happy as he had ever been in his life, but he had not forgotten his hero. When the first microphone was stuck in his face and the first television camera rolled into position, he looked into the camera, grinned his famous grin, and said, "Big Fella, I did it for you. I know your ankle hurts, but I want you to get up and dance."

Back in Los Angeles, Kareem, who had sweated through the whole televised game, covered his head with a blanket several times, and hobbled out into his backyard for air a couple of times, too, broke up with laughter. The next afternoon, when the plane carrying the team arrived back at Los Angeles airport,

Abdul-Jabbar was there to meet it. As he stepped onto the plane, the man in the first seat of the first row on the left stood up. "My man is here," he thought, and the two hugged each other.

Abdul-Jabbar was asked if he minded not being in on the victory he'd worked so hard for all season. "Not at all," he said. "In the Islamic culture we call that Kismet. Something that is fate. I was meant to be here, and Earvin was meant to have that game."

As for Earvin Johnson, he was so high from the game that he didn't come down to earth for days. But he knew he would come down to earth. All the hoopla would be over in a few days, he thought. Clowning around, he gave John Papaneck of *Sports Illustrated* and other reporters a sample of his deep-voiced E.J. the Deejay routine: "Goin' to Noo Yawk for the MVP thing, then back home to do some partyin' and play third base for the Number 1 softball team in Lansing—the *Magic Johnsons!* To be me, just plain Earvin Johnson again. Oh, maybe they'll congratulate me, you know, for one or two days, but then it'll be over. We'll be singing on the street corners again. This season—wow!—97 games. Exciting, crazy, fun. A lot of love for each other. A great experience. I learned a lot and—we're the world champs. Wow!"

Magic was wrong about the furor dying down after a couple of days. It didn't die down after a couple of days, or a couple of weeks, or a couple of months. Magic Johnson was the hottest news item in sports. No matter where he went, he was besieged by the press and fans.

He went home to Lansing not long after the championship series ended. Keeping his promise to his mother, he had enrolled in summer school at MSU to get more credits toward his degree. He was treated as a returning hero, even though the basketball team had not done very well that year without him. And the reaction at MSU was nothing compared to that of the town of Lansing. As Earvin explained, "In Lansing, most kids get out of high school and go straight to the factory, so I guess I was one of the first to kind of 'make it.' " Everyone was so proud of him.

At the same time, many of his friends and neighbors wondered if the year in the pros had changed him. After all, he was making all that money, had that championship ring and that series MVP award. He knew Kareem Abdul-Jabbar and had met all kinds of other famous athletes, like O.J. Simpson. All that could not help but go to his head. A lot of people were a little hesitant about approaching him, and it took a while for them to find out that he was still the same old Earvin.

But it was hard to be the same old Earvin when just about every sportswriter in the country, not to mention manufacturers' representatives and enthusiastic fans, seemed to converge on Lansing. Mrs. Johnson had thought her son's last year in high school had been hard on the family but now she realized all that excitement had been mild compared to this disruption of their lives. The Johnsons finally had to get an unlisted telephone number.

Earvin had made a lot of commitments. Besides doing advertisements for 7-Up, endorsing Converse sneakers and signing his name to Spalding basketballs, doing public relations appearances for his father's company, Oldsmobile, modeling Haggar "Magic Stretch" slacks, and promoting a Los Angeles pay TV outlet and the Magic Cookie Company in Los Angeles, he had signed on to do reporting for a weekly television series called "Speak Up, America." He was scheduled to do quite a bit of traveling around the country for on-location interviews for the program. And then there was his softball team. With his calendar crammed that full—plus going to school—there wasn't

Magic grins alongside his Most Valuable Player Award. *Wide World Photos*

Magic gives the victory sign after the Lakers win the 1980 NBA championship. Teammates Brad Holland and Kareem Abdul-Jabbar look on in approval.
Wide World Photos

much time for "singing on the corner."

Still, Magic loved every minute of his new life. Every day he was meeting new people, and next to basketball, people were his greatest interest. In fact, it seemed a golden time for him. He was young, he was rich, he was getting paid to play the game he loved, and he was winning at the pro game just as he had in high school and college. In fact, he had won so often that his coach worried that he didn't have a very realistic attitude about the game. As Westhead put it, "Magic thinks every season goes like this. You play some games, win the title, and get named MVP."

But reality has a way of intruding when you least expect it, reminding you that even in the golden times it is never far away. In the same week that the Lakers won the NBA championship, Terry Furlow was killed. The former MSU star—who had taken a junior high school player named Earvin Johnson under his wing—died when his automobile crashed into a pole on a highway in Ohio at three in the morning. There were traces of cocaine and Valium in his blood stream.

In many ways, Terry Furlow was a victim of the intense pressure of professional sports. Drafted by the Philadelphia 76ers in the first round of the 1976 college draft, he had expected to be a star immediately, just as he had been in high school and college. He could not adjust to playing in the shadow of Julius Erving. Traded to the Cleveland Cavaliers in 1977, he found himself in the same situation, couldn't handle it, and was traded to the Atlanta Hawks. By this time he had become surrounded by "groupies" who lifted his ego by telling him what a great shooter he was. Some of these people used drugs, and before long Furlow was using them, too. That did not help his behavior, and at the end of the 1978-79 season he was traded to Utah. He played well for most of the season, and on that basis asked for more money. When the Stars refused to renegotiate his contract, he began to use more drugs. He died at the age of 25.

Terry Furlow's death marred Earvin's joy over the Lakers winning the NBA championship. It also increased his determination not to make the same mistakes Terry had. He knew that drug use was quite common among NBA players and other professional athletes. He knew, too, that drug use was especially common in Los Angeles, where he lived most of the time. But he was not going to risk either his health or his career for some chemical high when he could get as high as he wanted to get just playing good basketball.

He was grateful to his parents and advisers for warning him about "groupies" and hangers-on. He had not really understood what they meant at the time. Now he did. Although it was his natural inclination to like people, he had learned not to give his trust easily, for there were people who would take advantage of him. This wariness had affected his relationships with women as well as men. "I really check out a young lady before I get involved," he has said. "If one catches my heart then she's caught me. But she's gonna have to work hard—just like I'm gonna have to do to catch hers."

There would be other things for Earvin Johnson to learn. One was that every basketball season would not be just "playing some games, winning the title, and getting named MVP." In his very next season Magic was seriously injured for the first time in his life.

The season began well for Johnson. He did not feel the same pressure to establish a reputation as he had felt during his rookie year. There was the new pressure, which he shared with all the Lakers, of being on the NBA championship-defending team. Opposing teams really got "up" when they met the Lakers, because beating the Lakers was a special win. But Magic enjoyed well-played, close games. He concentrated on developing his skills, like increasing his shooting range.

Twenty games into the season, the Lakers had a record of 15 and 5, and Magic Johnson had a very respectable personal record. He led the NBA in assists, with an 8.8 average, and in steals, with a 3.5 average. His average of 22.4 points per game placed him in tenth place in the league. He was shooting 53.3 percent from the floor and 79 percent from the foul line. He was the team's leading scorer and second best rebounder. But a series of mishaps cut short what Magic thought was shaping up to be his best season ever.

On November 11th, during a game in Atlanta, Tom Burleson, Atlanta's big center, fell on Magic while going after a loose ball. Five nights later, at the Forum in Los Angeles, Johnson and Tom LaGarde of Dallas collided. Both times, Johnson's left knee was hurt, and after the second mishap it really started to bother him. Medical treatments didn't seem to help, and he had trouble sleeping. But he continued to play. Then on November 18th, in the second quarter of a game against the Kansas City Kings, the Lakers were on defense and Magic cut to pick up the Kings' Hawkeye Whitney. Something in his knee popped or cracked and down to the floor he went. He hobbled off the court. By the time his teammates had sewed up the game 107-94, Magic Johnson was on the examination table.

The cartilage in his knee was severely torn. He would have surgery less than a week later. His left leg would be in a cast for another two or three weeks, and then there would be several weeks of exercising the knee and getting his whole body back in shape. According to the Lakers' team doctor, Magic could be out 10-12 weeks.

Suddenly, Johnson knew how his friend and college teammate Greg Kelser felt. He'd never sat out part of a season before. In the third game of his rookie season, he'd sprained his right knee, but he'd only missed a couple of games. Now he faced weeks and weeks and weeks without action.

He tried to remain cheerful. He told himself and everyone else that he would come back stronger than ever. But it was hard for an enthusiastic 21-year-old who'd never been seriously injured in his life to cope with a knee that wouldn't work anymore and a forced vacation from the game he loved most.

The rest of the Lakers were having their own problems coping—with the loss of Magic. It wasn't just his shooting and rebounding, assists and steals that they missed. They missed his enthusiasm. The Lakers, according to *New York Times* sportswriter Malcolm Moran, "developed an energy crisis."

Coach Paul Westhead put reserve guard Michael Cooper in Magic's spot, but there was no longer much magic in the starting lineup. Coach Westhead had to start shuffling his players around, searching for a winning combination, and naturally that caused hard feelings. To top it all off, Abdul-Jabbar was in a shooting slump. Although his shooting percentage of 50.5 while Johnson was injured was high enough to qualify most players as NBA all-stars, it was ten points lower than his percentage the previous season. For Kareem Abdul-Jabbar, it was indeed a slump. People started talking about his age and suggesting that he wanted to retire.

The Lakers lost five of their first nine games without Magic, but then they started to regroup. Jabbar showed that he was a true pro, and in the two months after Johnson's injury he began averaging about ten more points a game, and sinking 58 percent of his shots. The other Lakers rose to the occasion, too. They lost more games without Magic, but they stayed alive in the Pacific Division of the NBA's Western Conference. They never got more than about six games behind the Phoenix Suns, the division leaders, and they were still in play-off position. If Magic came back healthy, they would still have a good shot at their second NBA championship in a row.

Although he could not play with his team, Magic was often with them during the long weeks that followed his injury and operation. At every home game he was on the bench, cheering the Lakers on. But cheerleading from the sidelines was just not the same as cheering from the court. It was hard enough to keep up his own enthusiasm and not to let his injury get him down.

His rehabilitation treatments were a real chore. Six days a week he went to the National Athletic Health Institute in

Inglewood to exercise his knee. He would lie down on a platform fitted with weights, and move his legs in a bicycle motion against the weights. Each time the weights reached the floor, they would clang. Each time they reached their highest point, they would clang. Down—clang! Up—clang! Over and over and over. It was endless, and it was *work*. "Now I know how a factory worker feels," said Johnson.

The weeks passed. Magic's knee got stronger. But the first predictions about when he would be ready to play proved over-optimistic. He wasn't ready in ten weeks. He might have been ready in 11, but the Lakers organization was taking no chances. The team was staying in play-off position. The worst thing possible would be to make Magic play again when he wasn't completely ready.

After a few weeks, Johnson went home to East Lansing. His knee was now well enough for normal activity. But a professional basketball player engages in a lot more than normal activity. His whole body has to be in top shape, capable of enduring the grueling NBA games night after night. The next step in Johnson's rehabilitation was general conditioning.

Dr. Charles Tucker was in charge of that. At Jenison Field House at Michigan State University, where Magic had experienced so many victories, he did mile runs, sprints, and jumping drills day after day. To Magic's mind, even though he knew he was making progress, this wasn't much better than the "factory work" at the Health Institute. It was hard to be enthusiastic, even when surrounded by family and friends and with everyone in Lansing - East Lansing pulling for him. He never missed a workout, but he treated the workouts like a job—showed up on time, did his work, and left when he was supposed to.

By early February, Magic was beginning to feel like his old

self again. Dr. Tucker noticed the return of the old enthusiasm when he got to Jenison Field House and found Magic already there. He still wore a protective brace while working out, still put ice on his knee afterward, but he now did these things not so much because he needed to but because it was best to be on the safe side.

By mid-February, Magic was starting to condition himself mentally. In earlier weeks, while he watched a Lakers game on television, he didn't mind having other people around him. Now, he insisted on being alone. He'd play records and sit quietly before the game. Then he would watch it all by himself, projecting himself mentally into the square box and onto the court made up of airwaves.

Then he started to join his team for half-court scrimmages whenever they were nearby—in Chicago and Milwaukee. And at last, Lakers owner Jerry Buss made the all-important announcement: Magic would rejoin the Lakers on March 1, 1981, in a game at the Forum against the New Jersey Nets.

Overnight, tickets for that game were sold out. On the night of March 1st, many fans sported buttons that said "The Magic is Back." It was like Johnson's first game as a rookie—lots of hoopla. And Magic himself felt very much as he had before his first NBA game. He was nervous. He tossed and turned and dreamed about the game the night before. But he loved every minute of this positive nervousness—the kind that got his adrenaline going and made his hands sweaty and told him that he was back in the game at last.

The New Jersey Nets were at the bottom of the Atlantic Division and third from the bottom in the entire league. The Lakers did not want any more pressure than was necessary on Magic for his first game. They didn't even make him a starter.

Earvin Johnson of the Los Angeles Lakers and Marques Johnson of the Milwaukee Bucks fight for control over the ball. *Wide World Photos*

But he was the first reserve to be introduced, and he got a standing ovation. After 99 days out of action, Magic was back.

He did not enter the game until ten minutes of the first quarter had gone by. He was rusty. His first two passes became turnovers. Also, he wasn't sure how to fit in with the team anymore. He was no longer used to playing with the other Lakers on the court. The other Lakers, meanwhile, were not sure how to play with Johnson. This uncertainty on the part of the Lakers was quickly taken advantage of by the Nets. The New Jersey team kept the game close all the way.

With 9:53 left in the fourth quarter, Coach Westhead took Magic out. He'd played for 21 minutes, and in Coach Westhead's view that was more than enough for his first game in 99 days. But about seven minutes later Magic was back in. The announcement had just come over the public address system that Portland had beaten Phoenix. If the Lakers beat the Nets they would be just three-and-a-half games behind the Suns in the Pacific Division. At the moment, the Lakers were ahead by three.

Abdul-Jabbar tried to increase the lead to five with a skyhook, but he missed. The crowd groaned. Then the audience broke into cheers as Magic grabbed the offensive rebound. He passed the ball off to a teammate, who was fouled. The two free throws brought the score to 107-103 and to another Laker victory.

Magic finished the game with four turnovers and only 8 for 12 shots. But he also had four assists, and he'd pulled down a key rebound. He was happy, his teammates were happy, his coach was happy, and the fans were overjoyed. Magic was back.

He wasn't much older, but he was a whole lot wiser. He appreciated the game of basketball and his health far more than he ever had before. He understood that an unexpected tragedy could happen to him, just as it had happened to other people who had been close to him. He hoped that in the 17 regular-season games he had yet to play with the Lakers he could make a difference in the team's standing. He hoped that the Lakers would do well in the playoffs and become the first team to repeat as champions in 11 seasons.

The Lakers were not to achieve that distinction in 1981. They were eliminated in the playoffs by the Houston Rockets; and Magic had the unhappy distinction of being the Laker who took, and missed, the final shot in the final game against the Rockets. But no one held that missed shot against him. His taking that last shot had been a gamble—that hadn't paid off. But things could just as easily have gone the other way, and Magic could have been the hero of the game. In a game like basketball, you don't judge a player by a single shot but by overall performance, and considering how long he had been out of action because of his injury, Magic played remarkably well in the 1981 games in which he was on the floor, in uniform.

Lakers owner Jerry Buss didn't hold that missed shot against Magic. In fact, three months later, he signed his star guard to what was probably the biggest contract in sports history to date. Beginning in 1984, when Magic's current contract expired, he would receive one million dollars a year for 25 years!

Of course, Earvin will not be a player all that time. He expects to play for 10 or 12 more years. After that, if all goes according to plan, he will become the Lakers' coach or general manager. But he will be with the Lakers, and that is just where he wants to be in 25 years. Early in the 1980-81 season, before his injury, Magic asked Buss if there was any way to ensure that he would be a Laker forever. Sure enough, Buss found a way—a $25 million way. What else would you expect, with a man called Magic?

INDEX

A

Abdul-Jabbar, Kareem, 99, 106, 110, *111*, 113, 118, 122, 128, 131-36, 138-42, *144*, 148, 152,
Albert Schweitzer Games, 42
All-American team, U.S. college, *69*, *75*, 76, 91
American Basketball Association (ABA), 17, 97, 112
Andrews, Charles, 96
Artray, Dennis, *137*
Atlanta Hawks, 145, 147
Attles, Coach Al, 118

B

Barnes, Marty, 122
Basketball terms, defined, *See* Fast break; Man-and-a half defense, etc.
Battle Creek High School, 23, 28
Big Ten, the, 24, 50, 58-59, 62-63, 65, 72, 84
  defined, 61
  1979 title, 67-68
Bird, Larry, *34*, *60*, 91-94, 96-97, 133, 140
Birmingham Brother Rice High School, *15*, 39
Bonnie and Clyde's, 48
Boston Celtics, 96, 125, 132-33
Boys Club, 14, 18, 36
Brazil, 8
Brkovich, Mike, 63, 65-66, 73, 85, 88
Burleson, Tom, 147
Busing, 17, 20-22
Buss, Jerry, 108, 110, 112-13, 128-29, 150, 153

155

C

Cal State College, Fullerton, 82
Carrier Classic, 55, 72
Central Michigan University, 52, 54-55, 82
Chamberlain, Wilt, 13-14
Chapman, Robert, 51, 56-57, 63-64, 70, 73, 81
Charles, Ron, 53, 65-66, 81, 85, 88
Chastine, Reggie, *19*, 21-22, 24-25, *29*, 31-33, 36-37, 40
Chicago Bulls, 98, *137*
Chones, Jim, 110, 119, 122, 126, 136, 138, 140
Cleveland Cavaliers, 42, 110, *127*, 145
Cooper, Michael, 122, 136, 142
Coutre, Jim, 65, 70
Cunningham, Coach Billy, 140

D

Dallas Mavericks, 147
Dantely, Adrian, 106, 110
Dawkins, Darryl, *121*
Dawson, Paul, 28, 30, 36
Denver Nuggets, 120
DePaul University, 90, 92
Detroit Catholic Central High School, 23, 31-32, 39
Detroit Free Press, 66
Detroit News, 17, 28, 33, 36, 40, 42, 51, 67, 76, 87, 91
Detroit Northeastern High School 23, 31-32, 39
Detroit Pistons, 59, 66, 99, 122

Detroit Southwestern High School, *19*
Donnelly, Terry, 54, 56, 70, 73, 81, 92-94
Dwight Rice Junior High School, 16,

E

Eastern High School, 38
Erving, Julius, 133-34, 136, 139-40, 145
Europe, 42, 76, 82, 92
Everett High School, 17-18, 20-22, 25-26, 31-33, 36-37, 41, 43-44, 124, 136
Everett Vikings, 22-23, 26-28, 30-36-39, 42

F

Falls, Joe, 91
Fast break, defined, 59
Feldretch, Stan, 65
Fordson High School, 23, 28
Fox, Coach George, 16-18, 20-25, 27, 30-32, 34-41, 85
Frazier, Walt, 13-14
Furlow, Terry, 16, 24, 30, 42, 145

G

Golden State Warriors, *114*, 118

H

"Hardship," 74, 95-97
Haywood, Spencer, 110, 122, 134, 136
Heathcote, Coach Jud, 43, 50-51, 55, 58-59, 61-68, 70-72, 81-82, 85, 88, 92-93, 95
Hill High School, 23

Holland, Brad, *144*
Houston Rockets, 153
Howell High School, 38
Huffman, James, 39
Hunter, Larry, 28, 36

I

Indiana Pacers, 122
Indiana State University, *34, 49, 60, 83,* 90-92

J

Johnson, Christine, 11-14, 20, 25-26, 35, 74, 96, 105, 141
Johnson, Dennis, 118
Johnson, Earvin, Jr.
  awards and records, 27, 31, 40, 55, 59, 68, 73, *75,* 76, 140, 142, *143,* 144, 153
  basketball style, 14, 16-18, 24, 33, 56, 71, 113, 119, 126, 153
  and football, 16, 18, 20
  height, growth, 14, 16-17,
  injuries, 38, 118, 131, 146-50, 152-53
  receives nickname, 22, 39
  statistics, college, 68, 82
  statistics, high school, 23-24, 27, 31, 40
  statistics, NBA, 129, 140, 146
Johnson, Earvin, Sr., 11-13, 16, 26, 35, 43, 58, 61, 76, 96, 105
Johnson, Evelyn, 11, 27, 124-25
Johnson, Evon, 11
Johnson, Kim, 11
Johnson, Larry, 11, 13
Johnson, Marques, *151*
Johnson, Mike, 11

Johnson, Pearl, 11
Johnson, Quincy, 11
Jones, Caldwell, 138

K

Kansas City Kings, 76, 118, 147
Kearney, Joe, 95
Keith, Larry, 50, 81, 93
Keith, Luther, 51
Kelser, Greg, *34,* 51-52, 54, 56-58, *60,* 61-62, 64-67, 73, 81-82, 85, 87-88, 90, 92, 94, 99, 122, 147

L

LaGarde, Tom, 147
Lamar College, 87
Lansing State Journal, 22
Looney, Douglas, 97
Los Angeles Lakers, 13, 96, 98-99, 103-106, *107,* 108-109, 112, 117-119, 122-123, 125-126, 128-129, 131-136, 138-140, 145-150, *151,* 152-153
Louisiana State University, 87

M

Main Street Elementary School, 13-14
Man-and-a-half defense, defined, 93
Man-to-man defense, defined, 58-59
McKinney, Coach Jack, 110, 112-113, 115, 118-120
Michigan State News, 95
Michigan State University, 16, 36, 42-44, 47, 50-52, 63, 79, 81, 95, 141-142, 149

Learning Resources Center, 48, 80
Michigan State University Spartans, 51, 54-59, 62-68, 70-73, 81-82, 84-85, 87-88, 90, 92-94
Middle Tennessee State University, 56-57
Milwaukee Bucks, 110, *151*
Mix, Steve, 139
Moran, Malcolm, 148
Most Valuable Player (MVP), 1980 NBA championship series, 140, 142, *143*, 144

N

National Association for the Advancement of Colored People (NAACP), Junior, 36
National Athletic Health Institute, 149
National Basketball Association (NBA), 51, 59, 74, 90, 96-97, 105, 113, 125, 129, 132, 148, 150, 152
   1979 draft, 95-96, 98
   1980 championship series, 131-136, 138-139, 145
   rules, 103-04, 110, 112
National Collegiate Athletic Association (NCAA), 41, 52, 68
   1978 tournament, 68, 70-73
   1979 tournament, *34, 49, 53, 60, 83*, 85, 87-88, *89*, 90-94
New Jersey Nets, 126, 150, 152
New York Knicks, 13, 104
New York Times, 148

Newman, Bruce, 106, 122
Niles High School, 28
Nixon, Norm, 115, 120, 122, 125-126, 131-132, 136
Northwestern University, 67, 85
Notre Dame University, 36, 41, 87-88, 90

O

O'Hara, Mike, 17, 33, 36, 38, 40, 91
Ohio State University, 63-64
Old Dominion Classic, 59
Olympics, 95
One-and-one free throws, defined, 23

P

Papaneck, John, 153, 138, 141
Parks, Dan, 24
Payne, Coach Vern, 43
Penn State University, *89*, 90
Phelps, Coach Digger, 88
Philadelphia 76ers, 42, *121*, 125, 132-134, 138-140, 145
Phoenix Suns, 119, 148, 152
Portland Trailblazers, 110, 152
Providence College, 71
Purdue University, 84

R

Riley, Coach Pat, 126
Robertson, Oscar, 13

S

Saginaw High School, 39
San Diego Clippers, 117-18

Seattle Supersonics, 104, 118, 125, 128, 131-132
Sexton High School, 17, 22, 27
Shumway, Randy, 23
Southern Methodist University, 59
Soviet Union national team, 77, 82
Sports Illustrated, 50, 79, 81, 93, 95, 97, 106, 122, 135, 138, 141
Stabley, Fred, Jr., 22, 39
Syracuse University, 55, 72

T

Three-point basket, defined, 112
Tucker, Dr. Charles, 16-17, 20, 24, 35, 42, 61, 76, 95-96, 98, 108, 149-150
24-second clock, defined, 110

U

University of Cincinnati, 82
University of Dayton, 72-73
University of Detroit, 44, 56, 87
University of Illinois, 68, 84
University of Indiana, 36, 64-66
University of Iowa, 63
University of Kentucky, 72-73
University of Michigan, 35, 41-43, 65-66, 85
University of Minnesota, 61-62, 68, 84
University of New Hampshire, 59
University of North Carolina, 82
University of Rhode Island, 55
University of South Carolina, 124
University of Wisconsin, 68, 84,

Utah Jazz, 96
Utah Stars, 110, 145

V

Vincent, Jay, 14, 44, 51, 54, 56, 62, 64-65, 70, 81, 87-88, 90, 96

W

Waverly High School, 23, 26-27
Wells, Andy, 81, 95, 108
Western Kentucky State College, 72
Western Michigan University, 36, 56, 82
Westhead, Coach Paul, 120, 132, 135-136, 138-140, 144, 148, 152
Whitney, Hawkeye, 147
Wichita State University, 55-56
Wilkes, Jamaal, 106, 119, 122, 131, 134, 140

Z

Zone defense, defined, 58-59